Dare To Be You

# Dare To Be You

Eight Steps to Transforming Your Life

Cecilia d'Felice

© Cecilia d'Felice 2010

The right of Cecilia d'Felice to be identified as the author of
this work has been asserted in accordance with the
Copyright, Designs and Patents Act 1988.

First published in Great Britain in 2009 by Orion Books,
an imprint of the Orion Publishing Group Ltd
Orion House, 5 Upper St Martin's Lane,
London, WC2H 9EA
An Hachette UK Company

1  3  5  7  9  10  8  6  4  2

A CIP catalogue record for this book
is available from the British Library.

Typeset by Input Data Services Ltd,
Bridgwater, Somerset

Printed in Great Britain by Clays Ltd, St Ives plc

ISBN 978-1-4091-0652-4

To Henry and Hugo
My shining stars

# Contents

# Acknowledgements

The writing of a book is not a singular effort. Everything is made possible by the kindness, support, expertise, generosity of spirit and belief in others that we afford one another. Our creativity is inspired and nurtured by those who surround us. Although the words of this book are mine, I certainly cannot and do not want to take the credit for them. They could not have appeared here if it were not for the support I received from these extraordinary people who were so generous as to make it all possible and to have taught me what I know. I cannot thank them enough.

Dick Litton Holt.

Luigi Bonomi. Joanna Briscoe. Gary Brown. Tina Cartwright. Paula Conway. Rachel Davenhill. Anne Farmer. Melanie Fennel. Gigiola Fornari Spoto. Jeff Halperin. Helen Haste. Francesca Hume. Max Kite. Alan Lewis. Clare Longrigg. Clare Mallandine. Peter McGuffin. Stacey McNutt. Angela McMahon. Lucinda McNeile. Michael Mercer. Anne O'Brien. Charles Parkes. Matthew Patrick. Daniel Pick. Louise Randell. Alan Samson. Joe Schwartz. Philip Stokoe.

My beautiful friends and family: you know who you are, and I love you all.

All my patients, past, present and future.

The many doctors, surgeons, nurses and technicians who saved my life, not once but over and over.

My teachers.

*The Guest House*

This human being is a guest house
Every morning a new arrival.

A joy, a depression, a meanness,
some momentary awareness comes
as an unexpected visitor.

Welcome and entertain them all!
Even if they're a crowd of sorrows,
who violently sweep your house empty of its furniture,

still, treat each guest honourably.
He may be clearing you
out for some new delight.

The dark thought, the shame, the malice,
meet them at the door laughing,
and invite them in.

Be grateful for whoever comes,
because each has been sent
as a guide from beyond.

**Rumi**
(*Translated by Coleman Barks with John Moyne*)

# Introduction

Many self-help books start with an apology for adding another self-help book to your library and then tell you why you should make space for just one more. This one is different, you are promised, this one will really make a difference. I, for one, am not knocking them. I truly believe that in this life – the one we have all so miraculously been given – we need all the help we can get. I hope that this book might also help because it's not going to be about quick fixes, or anxiety-provoking 'must have, must do, must be' lists. This book is about life, real life: messy, awkward, uncompromising, disappointing, dangerous, haphazard, unknown and unknowable life. And isn't it good to be alive?

That old saying, 'we come into this world alone and die alone,' isn't really true. When born, we are tied to our mother with the cord of life; a perfect symbol for all the human connections that we will make in our lifetime. While it is true that we might die alone, for the rest of our time on this earth we are surrounded by people, for better or worse: amazing, unique, diverse people; all of whom have a story to tell. Some have done remarkable things, overcome incredible obstacles, survived extraordinary traumas, loved deeply and passionately, contributed their best and made our world a more beautiful place. And yes, there are also those people who hurt us, let us down, are cruel, thoughtless, and unskilful in relating to themselves and to others – and we can be that sort of person too, sometimes.

There are stories that inspire, repel, enchant, excite and compel. Whatever the content of the narrative, the extraordinary breadth of human experience is there for us to explore, so that we too can find answers to our own stories. What is fascinating is the process of life contained within these narratives. There is an indisputable multiverse of goals and steps, choices and coincidences, synchronistic encounters, potentialities grasped and lost and the happenstance of luck, which we can acknowledge have informed our progress thus far.

You might well wonder who I am and what I have done to think that I could be writing a book like this. I am a senior chartered NHS clinical psychologist working with adults experiencing emotional difficulties, such as anxiety and personality disorders, major depression, bi-polar disorder and psychosis. I study intra-personal (the relationship you have with yourself) and inter-personal (the relationship you have with others) relationships. I am particularly interested in how we communicate with ourselves, and the profound effects these communications have on our lives, shaping our reality.

In addition to my NHS work, in my spare time I offer relationship insights to the subscribers of Dating Direct and Match.com, the UK's largest Internet dating sites, focusing on how to make connections with potential partners that are authentic and meaningful and that have the capacity to be life changing. I also appear regularly on national radio and TV and write for newspapers and magazines, all in the hope of promoting this singular message: that we can relate to ourselves and others with love and compassion.

If we learn to do this, our lives change immeasurably for the better. It really is that simple. But the more difficult question is how do we go about doing it?

There are eight workshops in this book, designed to get us thinking about the world we have created for ourselves and the skills we can develop to overcome unhelpful ways of relating to ourselves and our lives. Some of the chapters are prefaced by some of my own most challenging experiences, and the methods that have helped me overcome adversity and suffering can perhaps help you too.

Much of what I have discovered about living a life I truly love has been learned through my own experiences and my continuously illuminating clinical work with my patients. I use the word patient rather than client, because I believe in the therapeutic nature of the relationship and that the overwhelming majority of people who seek therapy prefer to be called patients. The word 'patient' derives from the Latin, *patiens*, meaning one who endures or suffers. Emotional pain is no less distressing than physical pain and, left uncared for, creates chronic, sometimes lifelong suffering.

I am always struck by the bravery of every person who takes a personal risk and seeks psychological support. It is not an easy thing to admit that you are emotionally stuck and in need of help. Many of us are afraid of what we might find within if we do. We are often taught that we should hide our true feelings, manage them and not reveal them to the world. To take that step into the unknown, to admit to yourself and then to another that you do not know how to cope with your feelings and that you cannot make sense of them – instead of filling your life with meaning and pleasure, they fill your life with confusion and misery – is an admission few of us are prepared to make.

Frequently, I am asked what is it like when someone starts therapy, what actually happens? They wonder, 'What is the point? Can anyone really understand? How could therapy possibly help?' Often tearful, full of fear and uncertainty as to what therapy might 'do' to them, my patients tentatively begin to tell their story. For many, this is the first opportunity they will have had to describe their experiences to someone who is not a friend, partner or family member – someone, in other words, who can remain relatively objective and impartial. We do not know each other; yet we talk about the darkest fears and deepest despair that afflict so many lives. For some, the relief of being able to speak freely for the first time means that, once people start, they cannot stop. For others, it is harder to voice their feelings – as if there aren't the words to describe how they suffer.

In these early sessions, I am a historian; ravelling together fragile pieces of narrative to form a picture which varies in intensity and drama, but rarely is without loss, suffering and confusion. Many have been emotionally or physically neglected, have seen their families split by separation and divorce with little support or explanation, have been cruelly punished and criticised, bullied at school and work, experienced sexual and emotional abuse, or have lost a beloved parent, sibling or friend.

Some say they had a perfect childhood – as if to protect themselves and those they love from a less desirable truth.

Yet, often, they describe alcoholism and violence, or parents withdrawn into deep depression or confined to the house with panic and phobias. As adults they then find themselves depressed or anxious, as though they have learned to be that way, as if they have been shown no other option. No alternatives to living in this self-defeating way had been offered up, because in the midst of these singularly limited responses to life, no one thought to challenge or question what clearly was unworkable. Life – for many with this history – is relentlessly construed as a hardship, a cross to be borne, a punishment with someone to blame, usually themselves.

There is a sense of being trapped in a small confined prison, yet still feeling curiously lost. Part of my work is helping people to find their own way out. Once they have learned how to escape into a more constructive world for themselves, they are able to do so, whenever they choose.

Therapy can help us understand the past, but crucially, it is not about blaming the past – it is about trying to make sense of the present. Often, at the end of the first session, patients want to know my opinion. They want to know whether they are ill or having a breakdown, or simply going mad. What strikes me is how often they feel totally alone with their feelings, believing that no one else has ever had these experiences. This is perhaps what makes them question their sanity, since they perceive everyone else as being somehow 'normal', meaning they are able to cope with life with equanimity, meet all challenges head-on, without any suffering or self-doubt.

Therapy can help unravel the thoughts that lead to painful

feelings and self-destructive behaviours – whether it's drinking, drugging, spending or eating excessively, or other forms
of self-harming. Chapter 1 examines how our negative thinking can have an undermining effect on our relationship with
ourselves and how we can achieve a more balanced approach
to our lives. Therapy is not, however, a soft option; it requires
courage and commitment. It is not easy to face ourselves and
acknowledge that the way we have been going about our
lives perhaps has not been that skilful, nor to admit that
sometimes we have been unaware of how destructive our
actions and behaviours really are. This can feel horribly
exposing and feeds into our negative belief system that
somehow we have got it all wrong.

Eventually, however, there comes a time when we realise
that something has to change – that we need to do something
differently – if we are to transcend to a place where we can
start living our lives authentically. Chapter 2 explores how
it takes only three weeks to change unwanted behaviours
or thinking processes if we focus and discipline ourselves
skilfully. In Chapter 2 you will also learn that because your
brain remains flexible – whatever your age – you can retrain
it, priming it with new ways of thinking about yourself that
are both positive and life-enhancing. One of the basic tenets
of cognitive therapy is that we can learn to become our
own therapists. We learn to soothe ourselves by challenging
unhelpful thinking; reframing our experience so that we
unstick ourselves. This allows us to step into new possibilities
that include the ability to embrace the inevitablity of change,
so that we can choose to respond differently to life's challenges.

Chapters 3, 4 and 5 then offer insights and exercises into

how we can achieve that change and set ourselves free to live the life we truly love. We can do this without blaming ourselves. Instead, we can show ourselves understanding; learning to know ourselves deeply and to form a good relationship with ourselves that is at once loving, realistic and compassionate.

My time to change came in my mid-twenties, after a medical error nearly killed me. At the time, I made a pact with myself that, if I survived, I would stop hiding from myself emotionally and try to work out how and why I had become this person that I didn't know, didn't like and certainly didn't trust. I would look enviously at other people's lives and wonder how they were enjoying being themselves. For I undermined myself at every opportunity, questioning everything I ever said. I felt I had no genuine voice of my own, and that, when I did speak, the words were wrong and I was wrong. It was as if everything that came out of my mouth was to be attacked, ridiculed and condemned, not only by others, but by myself. I often found myself feeling confused, frustrated and disappointed, as if I had no life of my own.

Who was I? I certainly didn't seem to have a sense of myself that was positive or helpful. I realised that I needed to find an authentic way of being me, where I didn't doubt myself all the time, one in which I could be proud of who I was and what I stood for. I wanted to find ways to change my life, moving me closer to who I really wanted to be, while accepting with grace and courage that which I could not change.

I also wanted to experience psychotherapy for myself. I needed to do this to understand how I functioned emotionally, not just to know what it was like to be a patient for my own patients, but to allow myself to be helped in the way I expected my patients to allow themselves to be helped. I now know, after many years of first-hand experience, both personally and clinically, that good therapy transforms lives.

I do not claim to be an expert on happiness. I believe that the pursuit of happiness for its own sake is an existential red herring. Happiness is a by-product of other emotions, thoughts and actions which coalesce together creating a sensation of wellbeing. Investing in these other emotions, thoughts and ways of being will help us develop our capacity for happiness, particularly if we remember that it most often flourishes when we are happy with ourselves. As Matthieu Ricard,[1] a Buddhist monk, reputedly the happiest man in the world (although that is a title I suspect he would find meaningless) said, 'The basic root of happiness lies in our minds; outer circumstances are nothing more than adverse or favourable.'

Chapter 6 explores ways in which we can live our lives in the present moment, the most powerful way of achieving the state of mind we call being happy. Experience, and clinical practice, have taught me that emotional wellbeing is maintained through acceptance, compassion, resolution, altruism and humour. Basic needs such as diet, relaxation, friendship and exercise are also essential ingredients in promoting our emotional health and these too will be discussed in this book.

Although I have clinical expertise, I do not find it helpful

[1] M, Ricard, *Happiness: A Guide to Developing Life's Most Important Skill* (Atlantic Books, 2006)

to adopt an overarching 'expert' role: to be an expert suggests that somehow one has all the answers. When thinking about our emotional lives, how can this possibly be true? How can I know everything about you when I haven't met you or heard your story? In using this book you will become the expert on your own mind, developing what you really think and feel, and who you really want to be. My job is simply to signpost the way, using some of the best tools we currently have in cognitive therapy. Throughout this excursion, we can perhaps see ourselves as willing students, practising what is known in Zen Buddhism as 'Beginner's Mind' – always curious to find out more and to experiment creatively with the big questions, including how to learn to be ourselves and to love our lives. But I also know that this is not easy, not at all. We all need help because one fact of life remains incontrovertible: everything changes, and not always in the ways we expect it to. Chapter 7 explores how to develop the skill of living life with resilience and confidence, enabling us to weather the inevitable changes and challenges that we will continue to encounter throughout our lives. In Chapter 8 you will discover the gains psychology has made as a result of the fruitful work of Professor Martin Seligman and his Positive Psychology movement.

Using the steps that I have discovered work for me – steps that I hope will also work for you – I find that my negative emotions no longer propel me into a fixed state of unhappiness because I accept them as being part of my all-too-human vulnerability. Our emotions arise from the ancient reptilian part of our brain called the limbic system. They can be triggered automatically, such as with the fight-or-flight response when we are threatened, or they can be triggered by our thought processes. Emotions are meant to be fluid not fixed. Biologically, our emotions are designed to pass rapidly through us, taking about ninety seconds for them to flood through the body and then be flushed away in the bloodstream. Knowing that challenging feelings will pass helps us to look for fresh perspectives, to try doing things differently, and to take some risks.

Through therapy I have found that the more we understand why we choose to do the things we do, the easier it is to develop more skilful responses in making future choices. Choices that enable us to do what is constructive, nurturing and helpful to us, by knowing who we really are, not who we think we should be. Chapter 9 revisits a central theme of the book, encouraging us to think of ourselves without punitive judgement, allowing us to invest in the things that we truly care about and love, freeing us to live our life passionately, unafraid of what others may think, no longer at the mercy of unhelpful, attacking self-criticism.

In writing this book I hope that you will take a journey with me as we begin an exploration of what it is to be our vulnerable human selves, when all the old stories about who we are and why we are here begin to shift subtly as we embrace a new millennium. Many people reading this book will have been affected by the worst global economic recession of recent times. We have already discovered that there are no certainties; no guarantees that the good times last forever. It is essential that we learn to reflect, so that we do not continue to make the same mistakes about our economy, our ecology and the emotional wellbeing of our children and ourselves.

This book offers an exploration of the help that is available to us. Help that has been drawn from thousands of years of philosophy, hundreds of years of psychology, several decades of cognitive science and a handful of years from the new discipline of Positive Psychology. It is versed in scientifically evidence-based solutions for modern dilemmas. It is also written by a clinician and therapist, who having faced some of these dilemmas herself, found that these theories, ideas, techniques and practices can, and do, work.

*Dare to Be You* is a synthesis of therapeutic tools and techniques that you can apply to your own life. If you give yourself time to reflect on your many experiences, creating opportunities where you can challenge yourself, you will progress. You will find exercises, activities and cognitive reframe methods interspersed throughout the book. Please do not ignore these exercises. In cognitive therapy, those people who apply themselves to the personal work, keeping a journal and writing down their thoughts, feelings and reflections, tend to get better quicker and stay better longer than those who don't. You will need a large journal or folder to use in parallel with reading the book, as many of the exercises will require you to write down your thoughts and feelings. In this way you can chart your progress, revisit any work you have done in the light of new knowledge and generally keep a record of what works for you and what doesn't. Gradually, you will build up a picture of your internal world and how it affects your external world.

Life has a tendency to keep throwing things at us. This is the nature of our experience. Just when we think we have something worked out, something else comes along and we find ourselves destabilised once more by the tremors on our personal Richter scale. That's OK, it's how it is supposed to be and when those times come, it is good to know we have a resource where the work that will steer us through more difficult times has already been done.

Where possible I have used real dilemmas that people face, including those of my own life, breaking potential solutions down into step-by-step guides or exercises. What we are hoping to achieve is not a 'cure', but the creation of a fresh perspective, a new possibility, where we can begin to respond to our lives with an abundance of freedom, joy and fluidity. The more we can adopt a self-reflective, yet self-challenging position, the less likely we are to get bogged down in unhelpful, self-limiting behaviours that feed into our fear that nothing can change.

At the end of each chapter I will ask you to practise the techniques that we have explored, so that you can develop these constructive skills for yourself. Think of each week as a step towards transforming your life and each step as a mini-workshop. Week one will grow into week two, building on your skills as we continue. I will be asking you to practise these new skills for a minimum of three weeks to facilitate them becoming a part of you – a helpful habit, if you like, that will supersede, then make obsolete the unhelpful traps that we are prone to fall into when we do not take care of our emotional wellbeing. You will learn more about why it is important to commit to the work for a minimum of twenty-one days in Chapter 2.

I will ask you to work on three key areas each week:

- Your cognitions or thoughts, to help you develop clarity, a sense of perspective and to balance your mood.
- Your behaviour or actions, to help you become emotionally and

physically healthy because your mind and body are inextricably connected.

- Your emotions, where you can experience profound relational, spiritual or transformative experiences.

I hope to explore with you that daring to be yourself, your authentic self, will bring you the happiness and contentment you deserve. Whatever your story is, I hope that there is something here that will prove useful to you, and if there isn't, well pass it on to someone else who might benefit. Ideas are there to be shared and in this way they are given life. But, if you would like to create a beautiful, empathetic, compassionate and loving relationship with yourself and your life, read on – this book is for you.

# 1
## Challenge Negative Thinking

Low mood, anxiety and a feeling of being stuck are most often caused by what is known as maladaptive thinking. This type of thinking distorts our perception of reality and can trap us in relentless negative beliefs about ourselves and the world around us. As Shakespeare observed in the tragedy *Hamlet*, 'There is nothing either good or bad but thinking makes it so.' Or Milton's insight from *Paradise Lost*, 'The mind is its own place, and in itself can make a heaven of hell, and a hell of heaven.'

Let's reflect on this; what does it really mean? Simply, it means we are what we think we are. The idea that we create our reality is not a new one. Over two and a half thousand years ago, Siddhartha Gautama, the Buddha, is reputed to have said:

All that we are is the result of what we have thought; it is founded on our thoughts; it is made up of our thoughts. A man's life is the direct result of his thoughts ... We are what we think. All that we are arises with our thoughts. With our thoughts we make the world.

This quote could easily be attributed to a modern cognitive scientist, encapsulating the basic premise of cognitive therapy: that our thoughts affect our feelings. What cognitive scientists have discovered is that the Buddha, and ancient Greek philosophers like Socrates and the stoic Epictetus, were prescient when they determined that our thinking creates and defines our reality. We create the world we perceive.

Some people argue that there is an objective reality 'out there' that exists whether we are here or not and therefore the notion that we create reality is pure nonsense. But if we think for a moment about the world that we know and inhabit then although, yes, there is a concrete objective world out there that we can touch, feel and smell, this tangible world is constantly being filtered through our senses, creating a version of the world that is entirely subjective. Each one of us has a different experience of the world out there, because each one of us has a brain shaped by uniquely personal experiences, and these experiences form the picture of the world that we carry in our minds. In effect, we can think of our map of the world as being like a three-dimensional personalised hologram.

If we think to ourselves that we are afraid, a failure, unhappy, dissatisfied, a loser, mean, bad-tempered or uncaring, then this is the reality we are in danger of creating. If we challenge these negative thoughts and create a reality where we feel good about ourselves, that we are doing our best, that we care about ourselves and others, that we want to nurture ourselves and those we love, then this is also a reality that we can create.

To attend to what constructively helps us and leave behind

our doubts, there are some useful questions that get us thinking about what we bring to our world emotionally that affects the way we see it.

The first question asks us to think about the feelings we generally experience that give our day a particular quality, or colour. What feelings do we carry with us daily? Are they light, reflective, responsive feelings, such as joy, harmony, serenity, acceptance, tolerance and love? Or are they heavy, dark feelings such as despair, misery, judgement, envy or hatred, which leave our day feeling overwhelming and hopeless?

It is sometimes helpful to list on paper our most frequent emotional states, without censure. There is nothing wrong here; we just want to find out how we are really feeling on a regular basis. We can perhaps start by noting the mood we wake up with. Are we feeling sad, unhappy, stressed or anxious about the coming day ahead? Maybe we feel excited, fortunate to be alive and cannot wait to get out of the door to join in the fun. Or perhaps we feel calm, neutral, relaxed, without holding expectations about what lies ahead. Whatever our mood, we can note it and observe whether it stays this way for the rest of the day or whether there are interesting variations. Perhaps by lunchtime we are feeling more in control, or less tense, or perhaps, if our mood was good at the start of the day, we now feel tired and a little irritable. It is important for us to notice what has been happening, the context in which we find ourselves, and the effect this can have on our emotional state.

The more we begin to make these important emotional distinctions, instead of overgeneralising, the more we will identify triggers for mood changes. Knowing what we feel and when is the start of understanding that we can influence our mood positively. If we don't know what we feel, why we feel it, or when we feel it, then we cannot have a relationship with ourselves that is spontaneous, responsive and adaptive.

What is important here is giving ourselves the opportunity to document the variety of emotional experiences that colour our day. The more diverse the experience, the more in touch with our feelings we are. If our mood remains statically in the same negative domain all through the day then it suggests that there is something stuck or rigid in our responses and this will need looking at. The more fluid we are, the more our feelings move through us, the healthier we are emotionally. It is normal to feel happy, sad, angry, content, serene or agitated in the course of an hour or two, let alone a day, because it is through emotions that we process our subjective experience. They tell us what we feel about what is happening to us, and our emotional lexicon is just as rich and varied as the world that we inhabit.

The second question we might ask ourselves is how we think our typical mood state affects the way we perceive our world. If we are seeing the world through a lens of disappointment, mistrust, loss and hopelessness, then that is how our world will appear to us. We can be honest with ourselves right now, there is no one judging us, no one telling us that what we are experiencing is wrong. But it is important that we begin to acknowledge that our perception of the world is created by ourselves and no one else. Everyone has difficulties, everyone has loss, not one of us survives a lifetime without something bad happening. But this does not mean that our existence can only be about that very bad thing that has happened, or may happen, or even will happen, every single day, relentlessly and without variation. Yet that is sometimes what we do. We don't let go of the past; we cling to it in a *danse macabre*.

Changing the way we think is the most effective means we have to change the way we relate to ourselves for the better. Challenging our distorted thinking can help us change our mood, our outlook on the world and our future. It can enable us to become more engaged with ourselves and our lives. The tools and techniques that follow in this chapter are drawn from Cognitive Therapy, or Cognitive Behavioural Therapy (CBT) as it is also known. 'Cognitive' relates to the way we think and 'behavioural' relates to the things we do, our actions. We can harness what we know about challenging our negative thinking to help us create more effective, hopeful and inspiring thought processes that propel us closer to who we really want to be in the world.

It is worth remembering that, biologically, we are less thinking people who feel and more feeling people who think. Thinking constructively, therefore, can create a more helpful relationship with ourselves as we learn to show our feelings more understanding.

I was sectioned when suffering from postnatal depression after the birth of my first child in my early twenties. Like many women giving birth for the first time, I felt frighteningly out of control. The whole experience was not how I had imagined it from reading baby books: all so loving and gentle. Despite my request not to, my son was taken from me and bottle fed, something that often predicts poor breastfeeding as, unlike the nipple, the teat of a bottle requires no effort to suck. I lost confidence almost the moment I first held him in my arms and found I was unable to breast-feed him successfully.

My sense of failure was made worse by my son having a problem with his stomach, which meant he projectile vomited after every feed and often between feeds. When I tried to speak to medical professionals about it, I was told that vomiting was 'normal'. My son couldn't have toys in his cot or pram because he was constantly throwing up. I changed his sheets and clothing many times throughout the day and night, living with an unspoken anxiety that he might choke to death. It was heartbreaking to see him suffering in this way. Eventually, after months of catching vomit in my hands or scraping it off the walls and carpet, I received a diagnosis. Each episode made him cry pitifully and his little face and neck were constantly raw and sore. (He had pyloric stenosis, a congenital condition that could have easily been treated with medication to allow his stomach to function normally.) Meanwhile, I thought it was my fault, I must be doing something terribly wrong.

My critical internal judge came out with a vengeance, telling me what a terrible person I was. It took up a persistent low-level carp: 'You can never love your child properly, you can't even feed him, you are incompetent and useless.' I began to sink into a miserable state of self-recrimination and reproach. When my son was about three months old, my husband came home to find me in a state of distress that frightened him into irrevocable action, sowing the seeds of the end of our marriage. When I left hospital a week later, I felt totally worthless: my existence, pointless. I felt I had failed in every conceivable way.

The power of our internal critic can be devastatingly destructive. It can drive us to the extremes of our experience, leading us to self-medicate, self-harm, even commit suicide. To hear a constant monologue of criticism and self-loathing without respite, with no gentle word of nurturance or compassion, is to inhabit a truly miserable existence. Those who have not experienced depression can find it hard to understand – with good reason. Even those of us who have felt depressed find it hard to understand. We often don't know why we feel the way we do. Now I can see that I was suffering from postnatal depression, but at the time I was confused. I was supposed to be happy, but I was miserable. I was a good mother, but I thought everything I did was wrong. I was supposed to love my baby, but could only feel I was constantly letting him down.

There is no fact-sheet or instruction manual that guides us out of our distress; if it were that easy then depression wouldn't afflict sufferers for months or even years. Depression occurs in all sorts of contexts, not just when there are major life changes, such as the death of a loved one or the loss of a home, job, or social network. It can arise simply through the repetitive corrosive thoughts that chip away at self-esteem, self-confidence and self-love. If your internal critic holds dominion in your thinking, life can be painfully difficult.

Being sectioned was probably the lowest point I have ever reached psychologically. I seemed to be at the mercy of powers beyond my control, not just in my external world, but also the dark world inside my head that brought up every misdemeanour, every failure, every shame that belonged to me and repeatedly forced my face in it. My Catholic upbringing had consistently taught me that I would be punished, and deep down I thought I must deserve what was happening to me.

Being sectioned also meant that I had totally lost control of myself. I felt utterly lost and, worse, everyone now knew that I was lost. Sentencing was complete. My internal judge, black wool cap on head, had the court rise, and I was found wanting by my peers, by my family, by the medical profession. It seemed to me the whole world was my jury. My punishment was to be profoundly mis-understood, humiliated, condemned and imprisoned against my will.

But my real enemy was myself. My internal world was so hostile, so unloving and unforgiving that it propelled me to a place that I could so easily have not returned from.

In my role as a clinical psychologist, I have worked on locked wards with people who have been sectioned and I never forget my own experience. I know how frightened they are, how disorientated; how, even with the best staff and most enlightened treatments, patients are going to feel terribly confused and distressed. I have tried to bring com-passion to their experience, to comfort them and help them see that what is happening to them is the result of being on the extreme edge of emotional experience, and not that they are bad or mad.

Most negative thoughts about ourselves are not true. They are based on deeply held 'core' beliefs, which are often mis-erably self-punishing, such as 'I'm unlovable,' 'No one cares about me,' or my own 'I'm not good enough.' These deeply held beliefs are often learned early in life from messages we have received from our parents, teachers, other adults, our peer group and the losses and failures found in everyday life. They can also be construed from messages that our emotionally juvenile immature minds have misunderstood or distorted.

They can be based on fear of abandonment ('Please don't leave me!'), feelings of dependence ('I can't make it on my own') and vulnerability ('Catastrophe is about to strike'). They may be founded in the unrelenting standards we set for ourselves, which can be seen in my own, 'I'm not good enough.'

I know now that we do not have to fear what we feel. Our emotions are not there to destroy us, they are there to guide us and show us what needs taking care of. I made my desperate need for help into a problem, a failure on my part, rather than simply asking for the support I legitimately needed. If I could have shown myself some love and understanding, if I could have communicated what I really needed more assertively, I might have been heard in a different way.

We do not need to push our feelings away, or deny or obscure them with rationalisation or intellectual defences that isolate us. We can instead, embrace them.

It can also be helpful to relate to our internal critic with compassion. I often think of the voice of compassion as an idealised, internalised parent who, instead of telling you off when you feel you have failed, are sick or overwhelmed, picks you up and gives you a hug, telling you that everything is going to be all right, you are doing your best and that's what counts. This is the sort of parent that every one of us deserves to have. If we didn't have a parent like this when we were growing up, we can learn to create an internalised ideal parent for ourselves, now, as adults, by reframing our negative thinking.

Challenging our negative thoughts does not have to be about doing battle with them, which can easily leave us feeling defeated and hopeless. Better to start loving that part of ourselves that represents, in reality, how little we have loved ourselves in the past, and begin to learn to love ourselves now with a deep and healing sense of empathy.

To begin this process, tell your internal critic that you understand it, that you know where it has come from. Challenge the chorus of negative voices introjected from your parents, guardians, teachers, rule-givers, moral-coders, religious leaders and, most importantly yourself, for we are our own worst judge. Tell your internal critic that it is not actually helping you right now and you are going to relate to this part of yourself differently from this moment on.

The first stage is to learn to identify where, when and how your thinking becomes skewed or distorted.

There are three main types of thinking that influence how we feel about ourselves and our lives. Firstly, we automatically think about ourselves, our experience and our future in a negative light, and assume the worst possible scenarios rather than taking a more balanced perspective. Thinking in this way contributes to a general feeling of negativity that de-motivates us, preventing us from taking action that will make us feel better about ourselves.

Here are some of the more common thoughts: they are typical for many people, including myself. Note any that apply to you and add your own examples of the sorts of negative things you say to yourself and what you might say instead, experimenting with balanced and realistic reframes of these typical thinking distortions.

*Labelling:* I'm useless. I'm an idiot. I'm a bad person.
*Reframe:* I'm trying my best. I'm working things out and learning from my mistakes. I'm a good person who sometimes gets things wrong.

*All or nothing thinking:* Everything I do goes wrong. Nothing good happens to me.
*Reframe:* Most things I try work out OK. Lots of good things have happened to me and will happen to me again in the future.

*Fortune telling:* I'm going to fail my exam. I know they don't/aren't going to like me.
*Reframe:* If I work hard and concentrate I will improve my chances of passing my exam. I have good friends, which shows that when people get to know me they usually like me.

*Personalising:* My problems are entirely my own fault.
*Reframe:* Everyone has problems, that doesn't make them a failure or a bad person.

*Catastrophising:* It's all going to be a disaster. I have ruined everything.
*Reframe:* Usually things work out for the best. Doing my best is what counts. How can a small error really ruin everything? Most things are salvageable.

We might also hold rigid, punishing assumptions that are impossible to live up to. These are the 'should' and 'must' statements that keep us feeling trapped. Here are two of my own well-worn (un)favourites: *I must please everyone all of the time* and *I don't deserve to be loved.* Or:

*If I don't get that job, it means I'm a failure.*
*Reframe:* Many people will have applied for this job, getting an
    interview is a positive step forward and if I don't get the job
    I can ask for constructive feedback to help me in future
    interviews.

*I'm pathetic because I have problems.*
*Reframe:* Everyone has problems in life, that doesn't make them
    any worse a person.

*I will always be unhappy.*
*Reframe:* I have had periods in my life when I have been very happy.
    I can be happy again.

*I deserve to be miserable.*
*Reframe:* No one deserves to be miserable in life. I wouldn't wish
    that on my friend, so why wish it on myself?

Don't be afraid to recognise any other negative assumptions you might hold about yourself. It is only by acknowledging them that we can begin to challenge them. Sometimes we develop negative ideas about ourselves as a result of experiencing loss or failure. These ideas reflect negative core beliefs we might hold secretly deep inside, such as, '*I think I am helpless, unattractive, stupid or unlovable.*' Others might include the core belief that we are undeserving: *I deserve to be treated badly.* Or that we are a failure: *I'm doomed to fail.* Or that we need to seek constant approval: *If I am not perfect, no one will like me.*

Think for a moment about the negative beliefs you have about yourself and why you might have them. You will soon see that it can be difficult to do this in our heads. Our thoughts can quickly become confused, wandering off tangentially, leading us to dead ends, or they escalate exponentially, leaving us feeling overwhelmed. To enable us to unravel what is really going on in our thinking, it helps to get our thoughts down on paper. The next stage in this work does just that. Have your journal ready; it will become a friend to you as you learn to create a more balanced relationship with your thinking.

A 'Thought Record' helps us challenge or 'play with' the thinking that occurs when we are feeling negatively about ourselves. Making the record breaks down each problem or situation into three key areas: thoughts, feelings and behaviour. We can then identify the negative thoughts that keep us stuck in unhelpful ways of feeling and behaving. Identifying these 'hot' thoughts allows us to weigh up the evidence and establish whether our negative thoughts are true or not. We can then challenge the 'hot' thought, the one that causes us distress, and rationally reject it once we have checked out all the evidence.

It is also important to recognise what we are really feeling and not minimise the impact our feelings have on us. Having an authentic relationship with our emotions is vital if we are to understand ourselves and develop a skilful approach to managing our emotional world. Many people, when asked what they really feel, cannot unravel the sometimes paradoxical, conflicting emotions that flow through them, attempting to capture them in one-dimensional statements such as, 'I felt a bit annoyed' or 'I felt a bit angry'.

One of my patients believed that he often felt nothing at all when experiencing the negative thought processes that left him with a sense of being disconnected from himself and his life. As homework, I asked him to write down all the possible feelings that someone could feel over the course of a day. He came up with this amazing list, which I have reproduced below with his permission. Once he saw that it was possible to feel many things throughout the course of a single day, his sense of disconnection began to abate, as he was better able to make distinctions in how he experienced his emotions. Instead of feeling nothing or a vague irritation with life, he was able to extend his repertoire of feelings, which meant they were no longer lumped together in an unfathomable ball of undigested emotion. He discovered that he had learned to hide his real feelings over many years by taking on the role of family peacemaker. Denying his own emotional reality had left him feeling arid, emotionless and cold towards life. Instead of connecting emotionally with his partner, family and friends, he always felt at a distance, an outsider. This fed into his internal judgement that he was odd and different, unable to be spontaneously himself. Slowly, by taking time to process what was really occurring in him, his feelings came alive and he no longer felt stagnant and stuck. Giving himself permission to feel what he really felt, instead of what he thought he should feel, meant that he freed himself up and his range of emotions deepened as he discovered he did not need to fear them.

In normal circumstances feelings pass through us rapidly. We can experience thousands of subtle shifts in our emotional day, and this is healthy. It is when we cling to emotions that they become problematic, particularly those that are

negative. Making distinctions, identifying and acknowledging what we really feel, while understanding these feelings will pass, is essential if we are to develop a more
constructive relationship with ourselves. Here are some
common emotions that we can feel throughout the day:

*Accepted Affectionate Aggressive Agitated Agonised Amazed Angry
Anxious Arrogant Ashamed Astonished Avoidant Bashful Bewildered
Bitter Bold Bored Calm Cautious Cheated Close Cold Compassionate
Composed Confident Confused Contented Depressed Despised
Dignified Disappointed Disgusted Dismayed Dissatisfied Distraught
Distrustful Dreadful Ecstatic Elated Embarrassed Empty Enraged
Enthusiastic Exhausted Expressionless Fair Fed-up Frightened
Frustrated Funny Gleeful Gloomy Grieving Guilty Happy Hateful
Helpful Helpless Hopeful Humiliated Hurt Hysterical Insecure Insulted
Intimidated Irritable Jealous Joyful Justified Lonely Loved Loving Mad
Mean Melancholic Mischievous Needy Nervous Outrageous
Overwhelmed Panicked Passive Peaceful Pining Proud Provocative
Ridiculous Rejected Remote Respected Sad Satisfied Shamed Shocked
Shy Sorrowful Speechless Standoffish Surprised Uncaring Uneasy
Upbeat Used Vengeful Warm Withdrawn Worried Worthy*

There are, of course, many more emotions than these; can
you add any of your own to this list? I would add transcendence, vibrancy, *joie de vivre*, tenderness and self-doubt
as some of my favourite and not-so-favourite feelings!

Practise using the thought record (an example is coming
up) by writing down a situation where you ended up feeling
some distress. Then try to work out what it was you were
thinking that led you to feel emotionally and/or physically
upset, and record those feelings on the worksheet. Finally,

see if you can challenge, or if that feels too difficult, play around with the negative thoughts until you arrive at a more balanced perspective.

Remember, we are not trying to replace a negative thought with a positive thought – that would be unrealistic and superficial. Our aim is just to challenge the thinking that distorts our perception of reality and replace it with a thought that is more rational, realistic and helpful. Be patient: it can all look rather complicated to begin with, but the process of itemising and analysing soon breaks down the problem into manageable stages.

Here is an example of my own:

## Thought Record

**Situation**
Write down who you were with, what you were doing, when and where:

> On my way home from work after a long day, on the train, in the rush hour.

**Emotional and/or Physical Feeling**
Describe all the feelings you had at the time, whether they were physical or emotional or both:

> Exhausted, fed-up, uptight, stressed, tense, sad, irritable, impatient, frustrated, overwhelmed.

**Negative Automatic Thoughts**
Identify what you were thinking, the thoughts that came into your head automatically that caused you to feel distressed;

note how far you believe the negative thought(s) is true? With 0 = 'not true at all' and 10 = 'completely true':

| Thought | Belief |
|---|---|
| I can't cope. | 7 |
| I have too much to do. | 8 |
| Everyone else manages; I'm not good enough. | 9 |
| It's all going to go wrong. | 7 |

By capturing the thoughts and feelings, we are now in a position where we can consider the ways in which the thought can be challenged. The really 'hot' thought for me in this example is: 'Everyone else manages, I'm not good enough.' Having identified it, I can now do some work on it.

What is the evidence to support your negative automatic thoughts?

I feel tired and overwhelmed: that must mean I'm not coping.
If other people are coping, then maybe I am not good enough.

What is the evidence to refute your negative automatic thought?

You will see from this example that I play with the negative thought and explore several different perspectives, which enable me to understand what is really occurring and what needs taking care of.

I have just finished a really long day, worked very hard and am trying to get home on an overcrowded train. Maybe it's OK that I feel tired, it's normal.
Why would I think that meant I wasn't good enough?
Perhaps I am making a normal physical feeling of tiredness about failing.

I think I have a thinking distortion where feeling tired is the same as being weak, and weak = failure.

My feeling of tiredness is getting muddled with a feeling of failure and then I start thinking I'm not good enough.

No one else says I am not good enough.

I probably do have too much to do. I take on too much and then get overwhelmed. I'm not good at saying, 'No'.

I know after I have had a good night's sleep I will feel a lot better, so maybe it's more about being tired than I realise.

One of the most helpful things we can ask ourselves is, 'What would we say to a friend if they had this negative thought?'

My friend would say 'I don't think you're not good enough. You are feeling tired, it's understandable. You need a break. Don't worry, you are coping. Everyone feels like this sometimes, it doesn't mean they aren't good enough. It just means they are human. You are human too!'

Saying out loud or writing down the opinions that my internal critic uses to attack me gets me to confront what I am doing to myself. I can see how unhelpful, self-destructive and simply untrue many of these statements are. This enables me to regain balance. There is always an alternative perspective, one that has the possibility to represent kindness, care, hope and nurturance.

Once we have arrived at a more balanced perspective we can also activate something like compassion and self-understanding. People often say that they can be compassionate about others but not about themselves. If we understand compassion as the wish to alleviate distress or suffering, then it makes sense, if we want to be emotionally healthy, that we should wish to alleviate our own distress or suffering, particularly if our negative thinking is the root cause of that suffering. We can ask ourselves, is this negative thought really true? Do I honestly think this about myself or am I just having a go at myself? Is this the whole picture, is this all I can say about myself at this point, or is there a lot more going on that would be much more helpful to get in touch with? So in this example, I could say to myself:

> Don't be so hard on yourself. You are doing your best. Doing your best is enough. Allow yourself to be good enough, stop trying to be perfect, it simply doesn't exist. Trying to be perfect not only makes you exhausted but also makes you feel a failure. Let it go. No one and nothing is perfect. What you need is a nice warm bath and an early night to recharge your batteries and take care of yourself.

We can now take a moment to appraise how we now feel: have we arrived at a more balanced and helpful perspective? Hopefully we will have, because we will have challenged the negativity in the thought and come up with something that is less skewed and more realistic. We might want to score our feelings between 0–10, to gain a rational view of where our thinking now lies.

Score how much you now believe the negative thought is true between 0–10, with 0 meaning 'not true at all' and 10 meaning 'completely true'.

| | |
|---|---|
| I can't cope. | 3 |
| I have too much to do. | 7 |
| Everyone else manages; I'm not good enough. | 5 |
| It's all going to go wrong. | 2 |

My scores have come down considerably and feel more realistic. I can now see that I had made catastrophic predictions about my future, based on my fear that I am not good enough and this had sent me spiralling into distress, which was unhelpful. I also see that I still feel I have too much to do. This is telling me something important. I need to prioritise and say 'No' to things, perhaps delegate more so that I don't feel so tired at the end of the day. By doing the thought record I can challenge my maladaptive assumption that there is something terribly wrong with me and see my experience in its full context. I can see that I am tired and that rest will help me cope.

Try this exercise for yourself, exploring a situation that isn't too distressing so you can get the hang of it before examining issues that are more difficult. One of the most worthwhile things we can do when challenging our negative beliefs is to learn to be our own compassionate best friend. We can do this by asking ourselves what would we say to our own friend if they were saying these harsh things about themselves. We would want to comfort them, disabuse them of their skewed perspective and offer something more constructive and nurturing. Imagining what we would say to them in the same situation, applying a healthy mixture of empathy, understanding and compassion, allows us to access what would be good for us to hear. The more we can befriend ourselves, show ourselves the respect and love that we show those we care about, the more balanced, positive and supportive we can be towards ourselves.

As we discussed earlier, many of the dysfunctional thoughts we have about ourselves stem from deeply held but unhelpful 'core' beliefs such as the ones listed below. See how many you attribute to yourself; you may be surprised at your responses.

- I should be successful at everything I do.
- If I am not successful then I am a complete failure.
- Failing means I'm worthless and unlovable.
- Failure is intolerable and unacceptable to me.
- I have to get approval from everyone.
- If someone doesn't approve of me, it proves that I am unlovable or ugly, or worthless, or hopeless, or alone.
- I have to be sure of something to guarantee its success.
- I should never be anxious, depressed, uncertain, angry, sad or unhappy.
- Bad things will happen if I am not always 100% prepared.
- If people see that I am depressed, they will think bad things about me.
- Everything in my life should be wonderful and easy at all times.

You may have noticed other core beliefs or hot thoughts that you could add to this list. Try asking yourself what happens to your self-belief and your mood when you have these kinds of thoughts. Is this a world you want to stay in, or would you rather think about yourself differently?

You may have noticed other core beliefs or hot thoughts that you could add to this list. Perhaps ask yourself what you think happens to your self-belief and your mood when you have these kinds of thoughts? Is this a world you want to stay in, or would you rather think about yourself differently?

It is helpful if we think for a moment about why we hold

such beliefs. It may be that these beliefs are not really about us, they are about messages we have received that undermine us and we can reject them as the untrue comments they really are.

When challenging core beliefs it is always useful to ask ourselves, 'Why?' If we believe we must be loved and approved of by everyone, for example, we can ask ourselves, *'Why must I?'* In this way, we can start to establish the reasons for the way we think, to challenge our negative thoughts more successfully.

Eventually, these thoughts will no longer hold such dominion in your mind. You will begin to see that they are just thoughts that come and go, and importantly that they are not real. The more you dare to challenge them, the more you are daring to be the real you, who probably wants to be positive, gentle, loving and compassionate towards yourself, like a good parent or best friend would be. Staying in a world where we attack and condemn ourselves leaves us stuck, unable to grow emotionally or take risks because we think the worst will happen and that there is no point in trying to make changes.

Challenging negative thinking is one of the most con-structive things we can do to help ourselves. If negative thoughts make you feel depressed, then a more balanced, even positive perspective, is going to lift your mood. We were all taught at school that for every action there is an equal and opposite reaction, and in some ways it is the same with our thinking. Every negative thought, can, if we try, be replaced with something that is more constructive, more helpful to us and ultimately more realistic.

*

Cognitive Therapy takes time to take effect, and using a thought record once isn't going to make our negative thoughts go away. We have to keep practising and working to challenge them, because dysfunctional thinking becomes established over many years and it can take many months to create a more balanced view. But the effort is worth it, because every time you challenge a negative thought you weaken its hold on you.

When faced with negative thoughts and feeling stuck, there are three direct questions we can ask ourselves:

- Is this true?
- What is the evidence?
- Is this the only explanation or perspective?

These three simple questions can be applied to any negative thought that we might have. When you confront habitual automatic and negative thinking using these questions, you can create a different relationship with yourself and your issues. One in which change, growth and development can all occur. One in which you can take care of yourself and your feelings realistically. One in which you can choose to do things differently.

## Week One

Week One's exercises will focus on developing your ability to recognise the relationship between your thoughts and your feelings.

*What you will need*

A journal that is large enough to both write in and take pictures, cards and other inspirational items that you may want to collect while undergoing this process. You may want to use different coloured pens to denote your hot cognitions, emotional states and balanced perspectives. We can use these simple techniques to remind ourselves that we are undertaking a creative process in transforming ourselves. We are, after all, our own works of art, and acknowledging this is both nurturing and constructive.

## Cognitive

In your journal identify what your emotional default position is and how it affects your daily experiences. It is helpful to approach all these exercises from a position of openness. Do not edit yourself; be spontaneous and exploratory. There are no right or wrong answers; there is just you and your experience.

At the end of each day note in your journal all the different emotions you have felt during the day, becoming more aware of the many feelings that pass through you, sometimes moment to moment. Your aim is not to dwell on these emotions, but to begin the process of recognising that you are capable of many different feelings, not just an overgeneralised fixed sense of lowness or anxiety.

As an ongoing task, at the end of each week, ask yourself how your emotional relationship with yourself and your world is developing. Write down anything you have noticed about the way you really feel, no matter how small or apparently irrelevant. You should begin to see changes by the end of the first week as you become more finely attuned to the subtle shifts in mood that you experience. As each week passes, you will become increasingly aware of your real feelings until your emotional repertoire is fluid and supple, like a well-honed body. Do not fear that you will become emotionally unstable, for as you begin to make the distinctions in your mood states, you will see them more clearly and take care of them appropriately, rather than avoiding them or denying them, which usually ends up with some sort of emotional leakage. The more we know how we feel, the more we can take care of our feelings, which is where the thought record comes in.

Develop a powerfully compassionate relationship with your internal judge, one where you do not believe everything it says, and learn to show yourself empathy by reframing unhelpful thinking with more realistic responses. Be your own best friend or good parent by taking care of your feelings using the thought record in your journal, to identify your negative thoughts and then challenge them to create a more balanced perspective. Start with less complex issues so that you can give yourself a chance to get used to the technique, then you can tackle more difficult thoughts as they arise.

Use the thought record at the start or end of the day; simply find a time where you can be quiet and still for at least ten minutes. You can also use it as a way of coping if negative thoughts attempt to undermine you during the day. The important thing is to commit to using it, because it is a discipline, a skill that requires repeated practice to refine and master. The more consistently you practise challenging or experimenting with your thinking, the more automatic it will become. In time, you will be able to reframe your thinking immediately the negative thought arises.

**Behavioural**

After completing the thought record, do one nurturing activity for yourself. It is important that after completing each thought record you give yourself a reward, for in this way you will continue to practise this new discipline. It can be something as simple as making yourself a high-in-vitamin-C fruit smoothie or an antioxidant green tea (avoid caffeine, it is highly addictive and not an ideal companion when trying to make changes, giving as it does, a staccato-style energy that can activate the adrenal glands, making us feel jumpy and tense). It could be a warm bath, lighting a scented candle or bringing some fresh flowers into your home. Or try giving yourself a hug, by stroking your right hand gently down your left arm, from the top of your shoulder to the end of your fingers and vice versa, repeating the word, 'Soft, soft' as you do so. This has a marvellously tension-relieving effect, reminding us of how much stress we tend to carry in our shoulders. Whatever you do, make sure the reward really *is* a reward, mirroring your efforts to treat yourself with respect and love.

Your mind and body are not separate; they are, as I have said, inextricably connected and many cultures believe that an unwell body is the result of an unwell mind. Taking care of your mind is also about taking care of your body. Your body is not designed to be sedentary and if you are to transform yourself you must take care of your physical self as well as your emotional self. Every day this week go for a gentle ten-minute walk around your nearest park or wood, or if these are not available to you, walk around your neighbourhood noticing any birdsong, flowers, bushes, shrubs or trees as you pass by. Connecting with nature is vital for our wellbeing and a walk is one of the easiest ways we can soothe our mind, move our body joyfully and be close to the outdoors.

Throughout the book I will be encouraging you to take regular exercise so that you can develop emotional stability and have the energy to pursue your goals in life. Imagine your body as someone else's precious child that you have been asked to look after for the weekend. You wouldn't stuff them full of sugar, fizzy drinks, fatty foods, sit them down in front of the TV all day and not play with them. So why would you do that to yourself? Your body is your own precious child and it needs to be looked after. It is thought that two-thirds of adult Britons are inactive enough to be classed as sedentary, which has serious health implications. Regular exercise has proven health benefits, including an enhanced immune system, improvements in mood from endorphin release and protection against depression. Increase your opportunities for exercising by including activities such as gardening and housework, taking the stairs instead of a lift, walking up and down the escalator, and getting off the bus a few stops before home.

## Emotional
To help you understand your feelings, find sources of inspiration in art, music and literature. In your journal collect pictures, quotes – anything at all that gets you thinking about your emotions – scraps of fabric, colours, poems, leaves and petals can all be included in the mix. You do not have to be artistic, you can just begin to broaden your experience of the world by taking more notice of what is being created around you every day, whether by humans or nature.

Opening our minds helps us to open up to ourselves.

At the end of this week you will find you have already begun to think about yourself more flexibly, more creatively and more positively.

## Cognitive Reframe: Developing Compassion

Although some emotions can be agonising, they are a part of us that we cannot disown. Pity distances us from suffering, so feeling sorry for ourselves is never going to be helpful. Compassion, unlike pity, walks hand in hand with suffering. Compassion means acknowledging and understanding suffering, combined with the commitment to alleviate it. We could call it radical compassion: radical because it wants positively to influence the experience of suffering, to take care of it and therefore assuage as much hurt as possible.

Our internal judge is helpful when prompting us to apologise for things we have done wrong and we simply could not manage our lives without some form of judgement. But all too often this internal arbiter attacks us for no reason, telling us we are bad, unlovable, ugly and stupid. This voice is often generated by a fusion of our earliest critics, punishments and upsets. So, when we find we are attacking ourselves for no reason, when we constantly hear in our mind cruel and diminishing things about ourselves, we need to get compassionate. Why? Because we are in danger of declaring war on all our emotions to stave off this negative critic, unable to live with emotional authenticity.

To understand yourself and acknowledge that you feel both negative and positive emotions is to begin the process of compassion. Accepting that negative emotions arise naturally, as part of our humanity, allows us to see that they pass, as all feelings and sensations do. We can then allow compassion to step in and take care of these negative feelings. Compassion, remember, wants to alleviate our suffering, and we can do this by soothing ourselves, reminding ourselves that these emotions do not make us a bad person. Forgiving and nurturing ourselves, while trying different approaches to life that sustain our wellbeing, are all acts of compassion.

Many Western cultures see compassion as a weakness, as though it somehow prevents us from striving hard enough for success. If you have grown up in a family that does not value compassion, chances are you will have a harsh internal judge that tells you that you are weak and stupid for feeling emotional. Yet the reality is that it is compassion that makes us emotionally strong when we or those we love are suffering.

Showing ourselves empathy allows us to create a relationship with distressing emotions which is constructive. Instead of ignoring or denying painful feelings, we can gently work through them, accepting that they are a part of us. We wouldn't turn away from our door a friend who was suffering, we would welcome them in and try to ease their pain. We can do this for ourselves too, if we learn to empathise with our feelings and take care of them.

Learning to forgive our transgressions and faults brings us closer to having a compassionate relationship with ourselves and the world. By forgiving ourselves, we can learn from our mistakes and be open to new ways of thinking about our lives. Mistakes help us grow emotionally, especially if we remind ourselves that it's OK not to be perfect. We will always learn more from our so-called failures than our successes.

Opening ourselves up to emotional warmth generates

compassion and intimacy. If we can be warm with ourselves, our warmth will flow into others. Take a few moments to breathe in a sense of wellbeing. Imagine a crest of glowing light flowing through your body on the wave of your breath. Then breathe this warmth back out into the world, imagining it enveloping all those around you. Finally, try reading Paul Gilbert's *Compassion* for more ways to build a foundation of compassion in your life.

# 2

## Twenty-One Days to a New You

Neuroscience suggests that it takes only twenty-one days to form a new habit. This idea was first documented by Dr Maxwell Maltz in his ground-breaking book *Psycho-Cybernetics*.[2] This is exciting; it means that in less than a month you can replace an old unskilful habit with a new helpful one. If we do the same thing every day for twenty-one days, we can reprogramme our minds and create for ourselves the possibility of change.

This is a short chapter about how your brain works, which will help you to understand how to break down making important changes in your life into manageable steps so that you can develop a good relationship with yourself. 'Good' meaning healthy, nurturing, compassionate and caring.

Briefly, the brain is made up of several distinct parts, including the neo-cortex (*neo:* new, *cortex:* outer layer), so called because it is relatively new in comparison to the limbic system, which is the ancient, emotional part of the brain on which it sits. This is important to remember: our emotional

[2] M. Maltz, *Psycho-Cybernetics: A new way to get more living out of life* (Prentice Hall, 1960)

brain was there first. The neo-cortex contains two hemispheres, often described as our 'left' and 'right' brain, which
work in unison, unless the corpus callosum, the membrane
that connects both hemispheres, is severed. Our right
hemisphere controls the left half of our body and the left
hemisphere, the right. Brain scientists are able to distinguish
other functional differences in right- and left-brain activity.
The right brain, for example, thinks in pictures, experiences
the present moment, is creative, artistic, compassionate and
spontaneous. The left brain contains our language centres; it
defines, judges, conceptualises, stores facts and figures, and
creates stories. Clearly, there is a great deal more to the brain
than this, but for our purposes, this is a good starting point.

Our fabulous brains host approximately 100 billion tiny
nerve cells called neurons. Amazingly, each neuron contains
between 1,000 and 10,000 synapses. A synapse is like a dock
or port, allowing other synapses from other neurons to
connect through a web of dendrites – filigree-like structures
that allow for thousands of chemical reactions to spread
between the synapses. In this way these tiny cells can communicate with each other.

Neuronal connections are incredibly flexible and diverse;
with so many available docks for them to send chemical
electrical impulses to, any number of connections can be
made. These interconnections form networks called neural
nets or neuronets, also known as the brain's biological
wetware (think software in a computer). Every thought you
have, every memory you lay down, every skill you develop,
every lesson you learn, every dream you imagine is created
by a network of neurons firing together to form a neuronet.
Importantly, it is our emotions that heighten an experience

sufficiently that we remember it. In other words, emotions create the chemistry that reinforces our neurology to form a neural network that becomes memory.

The more emotional an experience, the more profound the memory, which is why we sometimes have responses to contexts and events that take us by surprise. When we were toddlers or babies, we might have formed neuronets associated with an event before we developed language, so we might find it hard to put into words why we have such a strong reaction, for example, to someone we meet later in life who reminds us of a past event. We aren't really feeling strongly about the person there in front of us; we are feeling strongly about what this person represents to us, laid down in a neuronet, which cannot distinguish past from present.

If the neuronet was formed and reinforced after we developed language, we can sometimes find words to express our feelings: 'I don't like this, it reminds me of . . .' I have never returned to mainland Spain, for example, not because I dislike Spain, but because I associate it strongly with a profoundly negative event which has unconsciously informed my choice of holiday destination. I haven't actively said to myself, 'I refuse to go to Spain because it was there that I went into anaphylactic shock when I was eight years old, and I nearly died', but when I look back I am aware that I have never returned since that time, despite having had opportunities to do so. Though I have always found a rational reason for not going, on reflection it's clear that my thinking has been informed by a powerfully negative emotional neuronet that tells me Spain equates with danger and so is best avoided.

The brain learns in two key ways: through repetition and

through experience. Of these, the most powerful and imme-diate is experience. If we think about it, this makes perfect sense. No amount of reading manuals about how to ride, sail, ski or surf will have the same impact as actually trying it out. All our experiences that have formed these millions of neuronets directly affect how we perceive our world. None of us perceive our world in exactly the same way, because all of our experiences are subtly different.

If you were raised in a large family with many brothers and sisters, your experience and understanding of 'family' will be different from that of an only child or someone who has just one other sibling. If you grew up never experiencing violence or abuse as a child, your understanding of 'child-hood' will be very different from someone who has. As an adult, your understanding of all that you have experienced informs the way in which you view your world.

It is not just our childhood experiences that have a bearing on how we perceive our world. Our brains are 'plastic', which means that they continue to develop and change as we age, forming new neuronets as new experiences arise. We are, therefore, continuously receiving data from our external reality, which we filter through our belief systems, our experi-ences, our imaginations and our sense of self. We are in a constant state of change, whether we realise it or not, because as new information becomes available, we have to make minute or sometimes massive adjustments to our under-standing of our world.

However, neural nets are not exclusively created, by exter-nal environmental events. When we lie in bed at night it is usually dark and quiet, so auditory and visual data are at a minimum. We are usually lying still; so kinesthetic data (movement) is significantly reduced, bar that of the pressure of our body on the mattress and the brush of bed linen against our skin. Usually there are few olfactory stimuli such as cooking smells to arouse us as we lie down to rest. We are left with only our minds. Yet in these conditions, when all our senses have significantly reduced data input, when the usual way in which we receive data about our world is shut down, our brains can be working overtime, so aroused and stimulated that we cannot sleep. We are busy creating worlds inside our heads with almost no provocation from the real world that surrounds us. Each thought we have lays down a new neuronet, and if they are affect (emotionally) laden, then they become more deeply ingrained.

Replaying in your mind an argument with someone at work will arouse the same responses as if it were happening in real life. Driven crazy by a love affair that went wrong a year ago? If you have been replaying that over and over in the dark recesses of your mind, the feelings provoked in you will be almost as alive as the day it happened. Our neuronets do not need an objective truth to formulate reality; they are blindly happy to accept any phenomenon that crosses your mind, setting up a complex process of invention, repetition and revision.

When events arise that trigger an established neuronet, our brain chemistry adjusts, creating an emotional response which further reinforces the neuronet, deepening the con-nection and directly influencing our perceptions. Each time a neuron makes a chemical connection through one of its many synapses with another neuron, it fires, linking the two cells, causing a multi-chain reaction that will in turn affect other cells, thus forming a net. The more these neurons fire with other neurons, the stronger the net they will forge.

Imagine this network of neurons firing together as a gossamer net: something fragile that can easily be broken. If we do not have a strong emotional reaction while forming the net, it will be a particularly delicate one, easily dissolved and discarded, particularly if the event does not repeat itself. If, however, the event repeats, the neural net will be reinforced; imagine it now as a net capable of catching a butterfly. If very strong emotions arise as the network forms, the net will require few repetitions to become strong enough to catch that butterfly. Repeated over and over, eventually the net becomes so well established that you could, metaphorically, catch a shoal of fish in it. It becomes an established memory (not infallible, however, because what we remember is informed by our beliefs, thoughts and feelings), but a memory nonetheless, and as such it will help shape our idiosyncratic reality.

Very simply put, neurons that fire together wire together. This is known as the Hebbian learning rule, described by neuropsychologist, Donald Hebb in 1949.[3] If we do something repeatedly, by the mere fact that we are repeating it, the process of learning starts to become simple and automatic. Repetition, as we all know, makes learning easy; gradually the action or skill we are trying to master becomes familiar, then natural and unconscious.

For example, if you usually look in the mirror and feel accepting of yourself, regardless of your physical attributes, you will feel good about yourself generally. You reinforce this by being compassionate towards yourself, not criticising or

[3] D.O. Hebb, *The Organisation of Behaviour* (Wiley, 1949)

condemning yourself and generally taking care of what you have. One day, however, you look in the mirror and say, 'Ah, not looking my best this morning.' You are having a normal and rational response to your appearance, acknowledging that you are not looking the way you normally like to look, without catastrophising what you see. Your established neural net is that you like and feel good about yourself. Your external appearance reflects to you what you feel inside. Your perception of yourself in the world is positive because your neuronet has established positive attributions that are, in turn, reinforced by how others perceive you, filtered through your own positive self-knowledge and the things you do to maintain a healthy relationship with yourself. This is known as a virtuous cycle, although more accurately it could be called a positive self-affirming cycle.

But there are some of us who, every day, construct vicious, self-destructive cognitive cycles. Instead of engendering a positive self-affirming relationship with ourselves, we create a powerfully negative emotional self-response, with statements arising in our minds such as, 'I am ugly,' or 'No one will ever love me.' Each time we say these words to ourselves and think negative thoughts that make us feel bad, we are reinforcing a neuronet that profoundly influences the way in which we perceive ourselves and our world. The strong emotional content of the thought reinforces the network until it becomes rigid. You could catch more than fish in this net; you could probably catch a Jabberwocky. This neuronet snicker-snacks every time you see yourself reflected in a surface. It flays away at your self-esteem, leaving you feeling increasingly raw and vulnerable. It becomes so inflexible that it doesn't allow any compassionate or caring thoughts to arise in you. You begin to think that this is true, that there is no other explanation: you really are ugly and no one ever will love you.

This neuronet is manifestly unhelpful, but you do not think to challenge it because it has become so well established that it informs everything you feel about yourself and your world. You have created a neural net so binding, so rigid that it forms a prison around your thinking, preventing you from seeing beyond into more constructive possibilities. Because only you have created this prison – albeit influenced by what others have done or said – only you know the extent to which it exists. Other people might sense it, reflected in your poor self-esteem and confidence, in the sad or worried look in your eye, in your downcast gaze or your pessimistic disposition. But only you will know just how bad it gets inside your head. Your neural network, reinforced by every damning, mean, attacking thing you have said to yourself, acts as judge and jury, condemning you to what feels like a life sentence. This sounds awful, doesn't it? Is there anything you can do to escape or does this mean that you are stuck here forever, in this unrelentingly undermining place?

Fortunately, all is not lost. Our neurology follows a logical path. If neurons that fire together wire together, then neurons that don't fire together don't wire together. The less you think the unhelpful thought, the weaker the electro-chemical reaction that passes through the web of dendrites – the afferent (conducting) structures of the neuron that link the synapses together. In time, the link becomes so weak that it ceases to influences your thinking; it no longer registers in your mind.

Remember that lovely friend you made on holiday and

how you promised to keep in touch, write emails, even made plans to visit? The strength of the emotional connection on holiday was enough to make you both want to stay in touch, seemingly forever. But over time, you send fewer emails, you go elsewhere on holiday and make new connections, and after a couple of years, you are only reminded of your brief friendship when you show your holiday snaps. What seemed like a strong connection at the time is weakened by lack of contact, lack of reinforcement and a lack of emotional content. Eventually the connection is severed.

In just such a way our neural networks can alter and change. If they are not being reinforced they will simply wither away until they are a distant memory that rarely surfaces. This is wonderful news for us because it means that if you stop thinking negatively about yourself, those old unhelpful connections will break down in time. If we do not keep investing them with our emotions, if we do not keep re-igniting them and thus prevent them firing together, they will eventually shrivel up and fade away. Hurrah!

The neuroplasticity of the brain is our ally. Because it can learn and unlearn, we can learn and unlearn too, even if we are older. The adage you cannot teach an old dog a new trick is only true if the dog doesn't want to learn. The one block to us changing is ourselves. And if we can laugh at ourselves, so much the better, because smiling and laughter affect the amygdala, the emotional part of the brain, encouraging us to be open to learning something new.

Many of us are reluctant to make changes because we have tried in the past and failed. We might have attempted to give up smoking or lose weight, and when we haven't achieved the result we were looking for instantly, we have given up.

Often the reason we fail is because we don't fully appreciate how the mind works. If we are trying to give up a bad habit without replacing it with something else, then we are working in an emotional vacuum – and that is rarely conducive to success.

Take, for example, a belief that you have about yourself that you want to shift. You start the week full of good intentions; your aim is to develop a more self-nurturing way of relating to yourself so that your body can benefit from the self-care and your mind can relax, knowing that you are looking after yourself. The first day feels hard because you have given yourself a difficult task, changing the way in which you relate to yourself. If you do not help yourself by challenging negative thoughts such as 'What's the point' or 'I'll never be able to make changes' with more balanced reframes, by the second day you are fed-up and will most likely give up. You may then feel disgusted with yourself for 'failing', and this will make you abandon all thoughts of creating a more nurturing relationship with yourself. Instead you will retreat into feeling guilty and remorseful. Feeling bad about yourself guarantees that you will not venture back into the world of self-nurture for a long time.

Preparing yourself emotionally for the change is vital because, if you remember, our neural nets are reinforced by our emotions. If you have prepared yourself for making the changes, your internal dialogue could be very different. Instead of rubbishing yourself for daring to think you can make the change, you could be saying to yourself, 'There is every point, I only have one mind and body and it is important to look after them as best I can', or 'I can make changes if I give myself small, realisable goals which will help me reach my target, such as exercising regularly, eating healthily, not staying late at work, seeing my friends and making sure I relax every day.'

The positive changes you are making will be reflected in the positive relationship you create with yourself by rewarding your efforts with encouragement. You are much more likely to go into the next day, week, month or year of your self-nurture if you are building intrinsic rewards into your approach.

Re-invention and renewal are available to us in each moment. The cells in our bodies are constantly being renewed. It is often quoted that it takes about seven years for all the cells in our body to die and be reborn; perhaps this is why seven is a lucky number to so many people – it is the number of renewal. Although I have been unable to find an accurate scientific reference for this, we do know that the cells in our body are much younger than our chronological age.[4] We are constantly being renewed and reformed. All of nature works on this principle. The seasons remind us that all around us there is a cycle of birth and death with all the stages of renewal in between. We can use this knowledge to our advantage when we apply it to our thinking about ourselves. When we find ourselves saying, 'I can't do it, nothing helps, I will always feel this way,' we can remind ourselves that this is not so because everything changes moment to moment.

Our emotions change because our bodies cannot sustain an emotional state for very long. Emotions expend energy

[4] K.L. Spalding, R.D. Bhardwaj, B.A. Buchholz, H. Druid, J. Frisen, 'Retrospective birth dating of cells in humans', *Cell* 122 (2005) 133–43

and the body is always trying to preserve energy, which is why an emotional release peaks, plateaus and then dissipates in approximately ninety seconds, unless we are highly emotionally charged. Our moods respond in the same way: eventually they have to change. If we think about how quickly one thought is replaced by another, often quite tangentially, it becomes very clear that our thoughts are in a constant state of change. Again, this is great news! If our thinking changes positively then our emotions can change positively too, because our thoughts create the way we feel.

When thinking about making changes it is helpful to break the process down into manageable stages. Reflect on each question and work through your answers in your journal. Revisit the plan periodically to see how you are progressing and whether you want to reassess your answers to the questions.

Begin by identifying the change or changes you want to make. Don't dismiss them out of hand, or tell yourself you will never succeed because your goal is too far-fetched or too out of reach. Let yourself dream of what you really want in your life. Step by step, from the kernel of your dream, you can then begin to move closer to where you want to be, by taking some risks, changing your behaviour and investing in yourself.

Breaking your hopes down into a series of achievable goals is the most constructive way of realising them. Even if we do not get to the top of the mountain, we will at least have given ourselves the chance to explore the foothills and, as we all know, the destination is not as important as the road you have travelled to arrive there. That is where the real satisfaction, learning, development and sense of achieve-ment come from: *how* you travelled, not where you travelled to.

*How important is change to you and how confident do you feel about making changes?*

When thinking about change, it can be helpful to identify just how important the change you want to make is to you. Then, when you come to make your plan you will have a good sense of the relevance of the change and the difference it will make to your life. Now assess how confident you feel about whether you can achieve your goal. If you are not as confident as you would like to be, all is not lost: think of ways you can elicit support from others. No change would ever get made if we waited until we felt one hundred per cent confident of success. We have to be realistic and work with what we have; for most of us, that means setting about making changes even when we're not that confident. The bottom line is, if we don't try, then we will regret not having taken the risk, not having a go. There is no shame in failure, but it would be a shame if we did not even make an attempt to change what we really want to change.

*How important is it for you to change this behaviour right now?*

Try rating how important you feel it is to change on the scale below by drawing an X on the line, where 0 means 'not important at all' and 10 means 'the most important thing I could do to help myself right now'.

0 _____ 10

*How confident are you that you can do it?*
Again, rate your confidence on the scale with an X, where 0
means 'not confident at all' and 10 means 'very confident'.

0 _____ 10

Do not worry if you do not feel very confident about making
the changes. You are being honest with yourself and this is
an important first stage. The more honest we are with ourselves from the outset, the more likely we are to achieve our
goals because we are coming from a realistic place, a place
where we understand we are human and fallible. If we have
a setback, it needn't destroy all the work we have done to
date; we just need to recalibrate and allow ourselves to start
again, knowing that none of our efforts have been wasted.

**Rewarding Yourself**
Rewards are intrinsic to achieving your goals. If you succeed
at step one of your change plan, reward yourself for having
done well. Rewards motivate us to continue. Making changes
is not a chore, a duty or a misery. If we see making changes
as being positive, life-enhancing and fulfilling, we will be
much more likely to continue with our endeavour and even
enjoy putting into place the building blocks that will create
new foundations for our lives. Foundations that will last,
that will bring us years of fulfilment and pleasure because
we made the effort and brought about changes. You might
even surprise yourself, which is always a good thing.

**Decision Matrix**
One way to work through the issues surrounding making a

change in your life is to use a 'decision matrix'. This is a way of encapsulating the benefits to you of making the change or staying the same, and the costs to you of making the change or staying the same. Those costs might be the effort you have to put in, or the discipline required to stick at something for that month or so it takes for the new behaviour to become a habit. By setting it out in a decision matrix, you might find that the costs of staying the same are outweighed by the costs to you of changing. Or you could discover that the benefits of making the change outweigh both the costs of making the change and the benefits of staying the same (which are usually negligible, if we are making changes for the better).

Each square of the decision matrix has a number. Start at number 1 and end at number 4, and you will end on a high, seeing all the potential of the changes that you want to make for yourself.

|  | *Staying the same* | *Changing* |
|---|---|---|
| **Benefits of** | 1 | 4 |
| **Costs of** | 2 | 3 |

## Making a Change Plan

As you work your way through the following questions, don't worry if you do not come up with brilliant, epiphanous answers. Go with whatever feels comfortable to you for now. You can always refine your change plan as you develop. The key to success is to start with manageable goals and realistic expectations.

## My Change Plan

- The change I want to see in my life is:
- The most important reason/s that I want to see this change in my life are:
- My main aims for myself in making these changes are:
- These are the things I plan to do to reach my goals:
- The first step I plan in making a change is:
- I aim to have achieved Step 1 of my plan by (continue with the additional steps you will need to make):
- Some things that could sabotage my plan up are:
- These are the people I could enlist to help me in changing:
- These are the ways they could help me:
- These are the positive outcomes I am hoping to achieve by pursuing the changes I want to make:
- I will know if the changes I want to make are occurring if:
- I will reward myself if I achieve the changes I want to make by:

Filling in the decision matrix and working out the costs and benefits should give you a clearer idea of what you stand to gain, and together with the change plan it can focus your mind on how best to approach your goal. The more friendly and undemanding we are towards ourselves when eliciting change, the more likely we are to get to where we want to go. If we are hostile, bullying or critical of ourselves we will very soon give up. Studies have shown that when teaching children new information, encouragement with positive feedback consistently achieves better results than criticism and punishment. This tells us something incredibly important about helping ourselves (and about teaching methods generally).

Humans do not respond well to punishment; it usually makes us feel hurt, resentful, inadequate and hopeless. When we are trying to learn something, being made to feel afraid of failure because we will get punished if we get it wrong can be counterproductive. If the amygdala, the highly emotional part of the brain, is flooded with fear hormones, it shuts down, restricting learning and processing from taking place. This is what happens in post-traumatic stress disorder. The brain, flooded by fear hormones triggered by the trauma, prevents the amygdala, the seat of our emotions, from processing what is happening. Undigested, the traumatic event revisits us over and over in flashbacks and night terrors, caught in a perpetual loop of unprocessed fear. If the amygdala is flooded with feel-good hormones from laughter, smiling and encouragement, it opens up the brain, creating conditions that are more receptive to learning.

When we are setting out to make changes, punishment and fear are not the stick and carrot that we require. In fact we don't want any sticks at all; it should be carrots all the way. Give yourself plenty of carrots in the form of rewards as you plan and make your changes! Rewards can be material, such as the money you have saved from giving up smoking being put towards a holiday; or they can be physical, such as the feeling of satisfaction you get from seeing your body get fit and toned through regular exercise. They can also be spiritual or emotional. We are not passive receivers of what life throws at us. Actively engaging in life – deciding how we want to live, asking questions of ourselves and trying to make a difference – creates a powerful shift in our subjective reality. The more we do for ourselves, the more powerful we feel.

Perhaps the most important reward, however, is experiencing your relationship with yourself change as you realise that you are doing something positive in your life. When we undermine ourselves, or do damage to our sense of integrity, we feel split and fragmented, weakened by internal conflict. Our sense of integrity is vital if we are to lead lives where we value and accept ourselves. Making changes and committing to them will boost your self-esteem and self-worth possibly more than anything else. That need to constantly seek reassurance from others will be replaced by the knowledge that we are OK because we're putting in the effort and we can see the results for ourselves. Creating a good relationship with ourselves is our ultimate goal, because from this foundation we can cultivate good relationships with those around us.

*How do you eat an elephant?*

There is a famous Indian saying: 'How do you eat an elephant?' The answer is simple and obvious: 'One bite at a time.' We tend to overcomplicate our lives and the way we live them. To make changes, we need them to be manageable, approaching them one day at a time or, even better, one moment at a time. If we hesitate or falter, we can remind ourselves that we do not have to throw out all our hard work in despair because we are not perfect; instead we simply start again, taking another bite. Starting again, over and over, for we have nothing to lose and everything to gain.

A useful mantra when making changes – and in fact in all areas of our life – might be, 'I can start again, in each and every moment, without shame, without fear and with compassion'. In this way we liberate ourselves from unrealistic expectations, unrelenting standards, unhelpful per-fectionism and our undermining critical internal judge.

Once we see that we can achieve change in a step-by-step yet enduring way in one area of our life, we begin to realise that the same simple plan will allow us to make changes in all areas of our lives.

## Week Two

**Cognitive**

At the beginning of week two, check out your levels of intention and confidence in changing your relationship with yourself, using the 10-point scale, and write up your findings in your journal. If your scores remain low on both counts, use the decision matrix to help you overcome your fears about making these changes. At the end of week two, review and note any changes – any movement at all – that indicates you are relating to yourself more flexibly.

In your journal, use the decision matrix to identify a persistent negative thought you have about yourself or a per-sistent negative habit you want to change, and calculate the cost/benefit of changing that thought or habit.

Next make a change plan, identifying your goals and how you will achieve them. Write it up in your journal and review it whenever you feel you need encouragement and support.

Continue to use the thought record every day, either at the start of the day, end of the day, or throughout, as a means of coping with persistent negative thoughts that pop up.

Note in your journal any activities that give you a sense of purpose, pleasure and/or mastery. The more you are able to identify the activities, pastimes, people and places that make you feel good about yourself and your life, the more you will be able to include these in your weekly schedule.

## Behavioural

Every day for the next week, look in the mirror and practise unconditional acceptance and loving compassion for the person reflected back at you. Instead of seeking out all that you feel is wrong, identify the things that you love about yourself. Do not feel embarrassed. Positive self-regard is a prerequisite for an emotionally healthy relationship with yourself. We are too aware of our shortcomings, worrying and obsessing over them relentlessly. We can be all too dismissive of our positive attributes – now is the time to focus on these. Say something gentle, loving and reassuring to yourself. Perhaps have a card by your mirror which affirms your intention to support and nurture yourself. Remember that repetition will build strong, resilient neural nets that will help you maintain your feelings of wellbeing and confidence.

Retrain your perspective to make space for being able to love yourself, not in a pathologically narcissistic 'I'm so wonderful and I don't care about anyone else' way, but in a way that allows you to make contact with your integrity, your values and your ability to care about yourself. Caring about the world around you will follow on from that. We know that those who are happiest are those who do most for the world, but they only have the capacity to invest in benefiting others if they are able to take care of themselves first.

Continue to give yourself a gentle, nurturing reward after completing your thought record and any of the other work suggested here. The more you build in reward systems, the more you will feel inclined to continue to do the work required. Work without reward soon leads to no work being done!

Do not forget your body this week. Increase your walk to fifteen minutes a day, connecting with nature. You should begin to feel your physical stamina improving. This week I would also like you to think about the fuel you put in your body and how you can increase your wellbeing through eating wisely. I give all my patients an emotional wellbeing diet sheet that I have adapted from Julia Ross's *The Mood Cure*, which I would recommend to anyone wishing to pursue the link between mood and food in more depth. The aim of the wellbeing diet is to optimise levels of serotonin naturally, without having to take medication.

Serotonin is a hormone that helps regulate our moods, making us feel positive and confident, with flexible and easy-going patterns of thinking and behaviour. Serotonin deficiency is believed to contribute towards negativity, obsessive thinking or behaviour, increased worrying, irritability and insomnia. Research has shown that serotonin reserves are depleted by stimulants such as caffeine, diet pills, cocaine and aspartame (also known as 'NutraSweet', and commonly found in diet drinks and foods). Serotonin reserves are also depleted by chronic stress and reduced levels of light exposure.

Serotonin is converted from an amino acid called tryptophan, which is found in high-protein foods such as free-range turkey, beef, pork, chicken, wild game, dairy products and eggs. Intensively farmed animals contain minimal amounts of tryptophan so these are not as beneficial to you as free-range products. It is recommended that you eat

20–30 grams of protein with each meal. Other sources of tryptophan include nutritional yeast, milk products, nuts, seeds, bananas and pumpkin.

By skipping meals you are likely to reduce tryptophan absorption significantly, so eat regularly. Serotonin production is also boosted by exercise and oxygen absorption, which is why your daily walk is so important.

*Foods to be avoided*
The following are implicated in lowering our mood:

- Sugar and refined sugar products
- Fizzy drinks
- White flour starches and wheat
- Refined vegetable or nut oils
- Margarine
- Any diet foods and drinks
- Any products that contain aspartame (NutraSweet).

*Foods to lift your mood*
All protein foods:

- Fish
- Meat – limit red meat to twice a week and view it as a side dish rather than the main focus of your meal
- Eggs
- Olive oil
- Coconut milk
- Vegetables
- Cheese
- Full cream milk

- Butter
- Whole-fat yoghurt

If you are on a dairy-free diet, try soya products instead. Supplements and herbs that can also help include:

- Calcium
- Magnesium
- Vitamins D and B complex ensure that neuro-transmitters remain consistently functional. Ensure you have enough of these in your diet or take a multi-vitamin supplement. Vitamin B complex supplements are particularly useful for soothing the central nervous system.
- Drinking camomile tea during the day and especially at night is highly beneficial as it contains natural chemicals that are soothing to the brain, and bisabolol, which is a muscle relaxant.
- 5-HTP is a close relative of tryptophan and part of the metabolic pathway that contributes to serotonin production. 5-HTP supplements are available from health food stores and have been shown in trials to lift mood.

Don't forget to consult your GP before embarking on any form of special diet with supplements.

**Emotional**

Continue to check in with your emotions. Practise taking your emotional pulse at set points during the day, using the emotions list in Chapter 1 to remind you of how many emotions you can experience. Notice how they ebb and flow, dip and lift, move outwards and return inwards. Your emotions are not static, they flow through you and the more you are able to identify what they are and why they occur, the more skill you will have in observing them for what they really are, rather than acting out on them and letting them bring you down.

Reflect on your progress in your journal. Notice any changes, however insignificant they might be, and record them. In this way, you will begin to create a log of evidence that supports you in continuing with your goal: to transform yourself by creating a more loving and compassionate relationship with yourself. Keep adding to your journal any inspirations that come your way.

At the end of this second week, find a time when you will not be disturbed, choose a piece of music that has emotional significance for you, and listen to it without distraction. Note your mood before you listen and then again after. Capture in your journal any feelings that arose in you, with the accompanying thoughts. Honour all your emotions, whatever they may be, then let them go. Music is a powerful mood enhancer and can be used intelligently as a way of helping us transcend mood states and move fluidly into more advanced levels of compassionate understanding.

## Cognitive Reframe – Worry

A classic stressor that drives our mood down is to worry about things that we have no control over. We are often so busy dreading events on our horizon that we prevent ourselves from enjoying the present. Projecting into an unknown future and catastrophising about the potential outcome is a classic symptom of anxiety. We can alleviate anxiety-provoking thoughts by challenging them head on, by questioning and confronting our thinking. Just as we did with the thought record, we can ask helpful questions to stop ourselves mulling over the worry and instead create a constructive dialogue around it.

First, what evidence is there to support your worry? Look for evidence that both supports and refutes the anxiety-provoking thought, because you are aiming for a realistically balanced view. Is there an alternative explanation for your anxiety? Try to find different perspectives.

For example, you worry that your report isn't up to your usual standard and that your boss will be disappointed. The evidence to support this worry might be that you had several other tough deadlines to meet that day and you didn't give this piece of work as much time as you would have liked. The evidence to refute this worry is that you often have to juggle responsibilities and this hasn't affected the quality of your work before. The balanced view is that, even if the report wasn't up to your usual standards, your manager understands that everyone is working to very tight deadlines and that it is OK not to be perfect, you can only do your best.

General questions to ask yourself might be: What would you tell a friend if they had the same worry? What would be helpful and supportive for you to hear right now? Next, go deeper and imagine the worst that could happen and then ask yourself if you could live through it. In the case of the report, for example, ask yourself whether you are being fair to yourself. After all, haven't you been working late fre-quently over the last few weeks, leaving you feeling a bit run down? It's not surprising you are feeling worried; you have a lot on your plate with family commitments, etc. A less anxious response might be: 'With so much going on in my life it's not surprising I am feeling rather depleted. I don't have to add to my burden by worrying about that report. If there is a problem, it can be sorted. Right now I am going to focus on my other priorities and make sure that I leave work on time so that I can recharge my batteries.'

Once you have confronted the worst possible outcome, imagine for yourself the best possible outcome, all the things that you can put in place to make everything work out well, all the skills you can bring to a situation that will optimise your chances of success. In this way you will get in touch with your innate resourcefulness and see that you are not powerless and you can regain control by identifying your strengths, rather than focusing your attention on perceived weaknesses. Finally, direct your thinking to the most realistic outcome, such as 'I know it is never as bad I think it will be', or 'the last time this happened things actually went well'.

If you still find yourself worrying uncontrollably about future events, another technique is to set aside some 'worry time'. This might sound surprising; making special time to worry feels counter-intuitive when you are trying to reduce your negative thinking. But a sixty-second worry break can be helpful as it provides a structured way of managing and controlling the amount of time you spend ruminating. Write your preoccupations down in a worry log. Setting aside a limited period of time places your thoughts in perspective. If you practise this regularly you will find that your worries will lose their power to frighten you. Checking back over your worry log will also allow you to see whether your worries have materialised and, if they have, how you have coped.

Worry breaks tend to show us that our worst fears are

rarely, if ever, realised. We also begin to see that the energy we have invested in staying attached to our anxieties could be used more constructively in thinking positively about our lives, thereby lifting our mood and raising our self-esteem and wellbeing.

If you are still worrying once the sixty seconds are up, try this visualisation technique:

Imagine your worries to be like drops of rain, one drop (or worry) instantly replaced by another. Then imagine putting up an umbrella to protect yourself from these incessant droplets before you become saturated with them. The umbrella is your awareness; your realisation that your worries are only thoughts, they are not facts, and that you are at liberty to think different, more helpful thoughts by returning your focus to whatever task is at hand.

# 3

## Freedom to Change

How do we create freedom to change ourselves? Freedom is such a beautiful and inspirational word, suggesting infinite possibility and choice. It is something that, naturally, we all say we want, but many of us are not sure how to accomplish it.

Take a moment to ask yourself what freedom really means to you. Be prepared for your answers to surprise you. Perhaps write down in your journal all the positive and negative connotations of what it means to be free. Note anything that you feel blocks freedom for you; note too, anything that helps to create a sense of liberation. What forces in your life shape your own sense of freedom? Are there boundaries or parameters that you have created that restrict your horizon? Do you hear in your mind stories from your past that construct self-limits like a picket fence around your dreams?

Exploring freedom is exciting, but also challenging because we might not have realised just how much we have limited our own potential to be free. Deep down we are aware that freedom is won through taking risks, risks that are both exhilarating and anxiety-provoking.

It might feel counter-intuitive to view freedom in a less than positive light, yet many of us baulk at choosing to live our lives as freely as possible, possibly because we fear the vast uncertain space that a truly free existence can afford us. Why might this be? 'We are the authors of ourselves', to quote Sartre, and with this authorship comes great responsibility. Perhaps this is a clue as to why freedom is something we all say we want and yet often find difficult to inhabit. Irvin Yalom, the great American psychotherapist, put it well when he wrote: '... freedom has a darker side. Viewed from the perspective of self-creation, choice, will and action, freedom is psychologically complex and permeated with anxiety.'

To create freedom for ourselves we have to acknowledge the risk involved and, while doing so, allow ourselves to step courageously into the clarity of expression that freedom affords. Our first task in embracing freedom is in losing our attachment to a belief that our problems are the result of things beyond our control, such as our relationships, our wellbeing, careers, genes, our parents or our lovers. When we can accept that freedom is the complete acknowledgement that we must be responsible for ourselves emotionally and physically, as best we can, we see that it is in *not* taking responsibility for ourselves that we lose our ability to choose wisely.

When we finally accept that there is no mileage in blaming others for the state of our lives and that in facing this truth we must nurture and take care of our thoughts, feelings and actions, we begin to inhabit a sense of freedom that allows us to grow, take risks and change regardless of the events that surround us.

Taking responsibility for ourselves is not about insisting that we have to do everything alone. Part of this understanding is to accept both our innate vulnerabilities and our need to ask for help. Freedom, therefore, is not only a state of mind; it is also a shared experience, one where we can invite others to join us.

To inhabit freedom is to inhabit love, discipline, responsibility and growth. This can be rather overwhelming, so if you feel you are coming up against blocks, pause and reflect on the limits you are placing on yourself. Remind yourself that creating freedom is about allowing yourself to step into new perspectives and new ways of thinking about your life. What begins as a challenge will soon become the most exciting adventure as you loosen up your self-imposed restrictions and begin to experiment with your life.

To help you begin this life-changing experience, here is a thought experiment to explore: Ask yourself, if you were free, who would you be and what would you be doing? Then ask yourself, without blame or judgement, why you aren't this person? Once we begin a truthful dialogue on the limits we impose upon ourselves, we can begin to embark on a different journey, allowing ourselves, as M. Scott Peck wisely said, to take 'the road less travelled'.

We often think that change has to begin somewhere else with someone else if our lives are to improve. We have all had the desire to change someone else, to try to make them more like we want them to be. We often feel that if only they could be more understanding of our point of view then our relationship with them would improve and all would be well. Mahatma Gandhi believed that we need to be the change we want to see in the world. This means that, instead of expecting others to change for us, we need to do the changing for ourselves.

While travelling in India, I met a New Yorker called Joel who told me that, having realised how terribly unhappy he was in his relationship, he had committed himself to being all the things that he wanted his partner to be: supportive, loving, kind, helpful, interested and thoughtful. He said that within two weeks his partner mirrored back all of the qualities that he valued and his relationship was saved. They are still together after thirty-five years.

Taking responsibility for our feelings and our actions is the key to making positive changes. By taking responsibility, we send out a strong message that we take what we feel seriously and act accordingly, by doing what is helpful, nurturing and compassionate. I call this radical acceptance, inspired by Marsha Linehan's[5] groundbreaking dialectical behavioural therapy, which encourages her patients to fully accept themselves and their world, as they truly are in the moment. We can acknowledge what is occurring truthfully, accept our feelings without blame or rancour and then choose to be the person we really want to be.

If someone behaves negatively towards you, ask yourself whether it's possible that you invite such behaviour, and if so, why. Sometimes putting up with a difficult or destructive relationship can be a way of re-visiting relationships from our formative years, as if we're trying to fix our relationship with our mother or father. Much as we might feel stuck, we're in a place that is familiar and therefore comforting in

[5] M.M. Linehan, *Skills Training Manual for Treating Borderline Personality Disorder*, (The Guildford Press, 1993)

some way. Many have found themselves in that situation and we know it doesn't usually work out well.

When faced with rejection, instead of acting out your feelings of hurt, anger or upset, try reflecting on why you have these feelings and what they are telling you about your emotional development. Let these feelings guide you to positive action; for example, by telling that person that you care about them but, in rejecting you, they are denying both of you the opportunity to work things out.

Our acceptance is radical, not passive, because in changing the way we habitually respond to something painful, we create the possibility that something different can occur. Instead of finding ourselves stuck in persistently unhelpful responses, we gently move into a more fluid, reflective way of being. This will impact positively on all our relationships, for this is an authentically powerful way of living, inhabiting our emotional truth while showing compassion for those we share our lives with.

After recovering from post-natal depression, I discovered an aptitude for motherhood that rescued me from the worst doubts I had about myself. I loved my boys with a passion I hadn't known I was capable of, and they loved me. I committed myself to motherhood – and then I nearly died.

It was twenty weeks into my third pregnancy and my bump was tiny. Someone told me I didn't look pregnant at all and I responded humorously, with a prescience that still chills me, that I must be incubating an alien. I had been to see the army doctor assigned to me through my former husband's work several times to question why I felt so sick, had lost rather than gained weight and why my tummy was so small at this mid-stage of my pregnancy. I was told not to worry about it, but later, at a routine check-up, the midwife told me there was no foetal heartbeat and an immediate appointment was made for me to see a radiologist in our local hospital. Panic set in; I was upset and confused, and remember driving rather dramatically through a military checkpoint to collect my husband from his army base with the soldier on guard running after the car waving his rifle at me because I hadn't registered at the reporting desk. I was too anxious to stop; I needed to get to the hospital and I couldn't face doing it alone.

I was told that there was no baby. After twenty weeks of feeling pregnant, having permanent morning sickness, even having milk in my breasts, this seemed inconceivable. Looking at the monitor, all I could see was a snowstorm of confusion. Crushingly, there really was no baby, and a wave of oily nausea hit me as my worst fears were realised. I was ushered to a room and told to wait until a doctor could come and see me. An anxious, pale-looking woman arrived sometime later to tell me that I had something called a hydatidiform mole pregnancy. This meant that, although an embryo had formed, early on in the pregnancy it had become engulfed by a potentially cancerous tumour – the mole – that destroyed the embryo while still producing human growth hormone. This is why I continued to manifest a pregnancy even though the foetus was long dead. The treatment involved having a radical scrape of my uterus to remove any traces of the tumour and then to have follow-up treatment with the oncology department of a London hospital to ensure that cancer was not developing or spreading. I was told that this procedure was very safe, there was no need to worry and that I would be operated on quickly, placed on the surgical list at the end of the next day.

It was awful, to lose my baby that in my mind was halfway to being born and to have instead a tumour, the alien of my worried thoughts, lurking in the very core of me, where life should be. I felt invaded and that distant sense that I was harbouring something sinister inside my body rapidly intensified, making me feel repellent. I didn't want anyone to touch me, I felt contaminated and longed for this revolting growth to be removed.

Coming round from the anaesthetic alone, I felt a terrible pain in my abdomen and weakly rang for a nurse to ask for painkillers. I was told firmly that I should not be feeling pain because I had only had a scrape, which couldn't possibly hurt. I was confused, I was in terrible pain but wasn't supposed to be and decided it was probably better to say nothing. Feeling drained, I went home, glad that it was over. I tried not to think about what had happened; it felt so disturbing and, again in my mind, pointed to my failure as a woman. I couldn't even get a pregnancy right.

After leaving hospital, I continued to have moments when I would suddenly feel excruciating pain in my right abdomen as if something was severely bruising me from the inside. Occasionally, I would collapse, doubled up in pain. The third time this happened, I called the hospital and asked to speak to my gynaecologist. I was told that I wasn't 'allowed to', as if I was merely an irritating child; I could only speak to him if it was a matter of life and death, and as this clearly wasn't, the female doctor said, I had to wait for my next scheduled appointment.

I thought something was terribly wrong, much as I had known something had been wrong with the pregnancy all along, but I didn't know what to say or do. After all, what did I know? They were the experts and I, young and woefully lacking in confidence, believed that I must be nothing but a neurotic hypchondriac.

A few weeks later, as part of my follow-up treatment for the hydatidiform mole pregnancy, I had to have X-rays taken to ensure cancer hadn't spread to my lungs. A radiographer also scanned my abdomen to look for changes in my uterus. To my dismay, the radiographer took a sharp intake of breath, rather as the previous radiographer had on finding the tumour. I prepared myself for more bad news. There was a large growth. It looked as if it was on the right ovary, very odd and possibly cancerous. I should be seen by my gynaecologist immediately.

After a surprisingly painful internal examination, my kind gynaecologist told me that they would need to open me up to have a look around, as he not sure what was going on. It was a routine procedure and nothing to worry about. However, I was beginning to learn that nothing is straightforward when it comes to doctors and surgery. Later that day, after the laparoscopy, I came to, lying in a room on my own and feeling very strange: I can only describe it as if someone had pulled the plug on me. This feeling of total collapse, despite lying down, was so intense that I rang the emergency bell. I remember thinking; I *have* to ring the bell. Now.

Immediately, a nurse arrived and on seeing me she blanched. I didn't know what she had seen in me, but without speaking, she tipped my bed by 45 degrees so my head was below my feet and ran out of the room for help. The next moment I was wet with warm blood. It trickled down the bed, creeping up my back into the nape of my neck, collecting in my ears and hair. I looked down the length of my body; between my legs, the white sheets were now darkly saturated. I looked away, unable to register what was happening. By now the blood was seeping everywhere and the pain that I had felt earlier intensified. It came in sickening waves, and soon I became aware that the pain signified large clots of blood leaving my body. Even then I didn't know how. I had no idea what was happening to me, none at all, except I was bleeding.

I was in so much generalised pain that I could not discern how this blood was escaping so violently. Some clots were so massive they needed two hands to pick them up. I must have kept blacking out because what I saw next was a room full of medical staff. Nurses were scooping blood into bowls so that it could be weighed to see how much was being lost. Doctors were attaching me to units of blood, two bags for each arm. Periodically, my veins would suddenly collapse and a new line would be sought, the nurses squeezing the bags to force the blood into my body more and more urgently.

I had no idea that blood could drain so quickly and painfully from a body. I had no idea that I had so much blood to lose. Eight pints or so: it doesn't sound such a lot in an adult frame, but seeing it spread out on the bed around me, dripping off the edges on to the floor, being scraped up by anxious nurses, blood covering their arms, their cloudy thin plastic aprons, wiped across their faces, was more than alarming. In fact, I cannot really express in words how terribly frightening it was.

Throughout the day, I continued to haemorrhage and lose consciousness. Those first eight pints had long been replaced and I was by now well into double figures of the transfusion. My arms and hands began to swell like balloons. A senior anaesthetist was summoned to try and find a vein to attach another line to; four bags at a time was not enough. It was hard to tell where I stopped and the blood began. This blood was no longer mine, it belonged to other people; kind people, people who had given something of themselves for nothing: altruistic, loving, unknown people. People I owe my life to.

The sheets long removed, I lay on the pale blue mattress, now red and sticky. Occasionally, the blood would clot and stop flowing, only to start again with renewed force. I became increasingly weak; life-support equipment was moved into my room and I stayed more out of consciousness than in. I could feel myself, like a tired cliché, 'slipping away', caring less and less whether I survived. More and more I just wanted it to be over. Sometimes I would wake up to hear whispering outside my room, saying that I wouldn't make it, or discussing the surgeon who had done the 'mess up', and that they should operate on me before it was 'too late'. In my hazy, weakened mind, I refused to believe they were talking about me, convinced they were talking about someone else, such is the power of denial.

At about four the following morning the doctors decided that I would not survive another bleed. I was rushed down to surgery, wheeled into the operating theatre still conscious, so frail that I had to be placed on life support before they could anaesthetise me. I still vividly remember the green masked faces of the surgical team, woken from their beds before dawn. I attempted to murmur an apology for getting them up and thank them for being there, but they didn't hear me, my voice had withered to wordless rasps. All I could see was their scared eyes behind the reassuringly professional expressions they were trying to assume. One of them squeezed my hand and told me not to worry, probably as much for their own benefit as for mine; the tension was palpable.

Lying there, I really didn't think I would make it. Was this how it was supposed to be? Some bad things had happened to me in the past, but this seemed extraordinarily unlucky. The feelings were strange and confusing; I didn't want to die, but I also knew I couldn't take any more transfusions. There had been times when, drifting into unconsciousness, I hoped I wouldn't wake up again. I was so exhausted by it all – the sea of blood, the agonising pain, but most of all the terrible, terrible fear that either it would never end or that it would for the worst possible reason. Thinking of my children was both agonising, as I contemplated never seeing them again, and inspiring, keeping me clinging on to life in the hope that I would.

Until then, I had never understood why people gave up the will to live, why they got too tired of suffering to continue. I always thought that, whatever happened, you would go on struggling to the very end. Now I knew how hard it could be to keep going, to keep up the fight, to force yourself to survive. More than anything, I just wanted it to stop, in whatever form that took, but that made me feel terribly frightened and I wanted that to stop too.

Lying there in surgery, knowing I didn't really want to die, I attempted to summon up the strength to fight on, but I felt so fragile. My body seemed hollowed out and desiccated, a rattling space where once substance had been. It was as if with every corpuscle lost, part of me had been lost too; my thoughts and feelings were becoming increasingly obscured and indistinct, as if I no longer figured in my own life.

Overwhelming fear consumed me and I knew I had to say farewell to my beloved babies in my mind before I died. Picturing them, their dear little faces, their beautiful smiles, their tears and laughter, I suddenly remembered we had a future together. A future that I longed to be able to share, a future that embodied hope that I could continue to love them. Just before the anaesthetic took me, I had no choice but to reconnect with my desire to live, to be with them and see them grow up. They needed their mother. It was that simple. I had to get through this for them. Too late, like a character in a book, I started to make promises, a desperate pact to cheat death and live. But my promises, as yet vague and unformed, drifted hopelessly away from me as I fell into nothingness.

I was in surgery for over five hours. At some point they must have been trying to revive me because I remember being in terrible pain and hearing my name being called. It sounded eerily like a Kate Bush record that had got stuck in an interminable groove: instead of 'Cathy,' she was singing my name in falsetto. Much as I adore Kate Bush and was glad she seemed to be calling for me, this was agonisingly repetitive, like a hideous torture, and combined with the bizarre morphine-induced geometric shapes spinning nauseatingly in my mind's eye, I decided I must be dead, languishing in the ironic purgatory of my Catholic education.

Gradually I became aware that Kate had stopped screeching my name. Relief! Time was so distorted as to be unrecognisable. I didn't know if I had been there for five minutes or five thousand years. Where I began and ended was indefinable: I no longer seemed to have a body, but I had some sort of a mind and it was full of exquisite pain. I felt as though I was dark and bottomless, without form, more a cloud of blackness, where the I that is me seemed to have dissolved into nothingness. I waited for something to happen. How long would I stay in this place?

Gradually, I had a sinister sensation that I was not alone. It was then that I realised, to my soundless horror, that the darkness that I had now become was inhabited by the souls of thousands of equally amorphous dead babies. Unbaptised babies; condemned to languish by a Church that purported to praise a merciful God. It was an abomination. I felt I could do nothing to comfort these innocent wraiths, trapped like me in a Stygian hell, and it was then that I felt completely and genuinely without hope for the first time in my experience. There was no light, texture or sound; nothing that could help me identify whether I was still alive or not; and if dead, then my fate was surely to share eternity with these tragic infants.

Then once again, morphine-mad monochrome geometric shapes loomed in and out of the blackness, spiralling maniacally as if to slice the me, who was strangely missing, into dismal shreds. The babies were beginning to cry. We were drowning in all the sorrows of the world and there appeared to be no reprieve.

Mercifully, this seemingly indefinite miserable existence suddenly stopped, as I fell again into unconsciousness. Then there was nothing for a long time. This phenomenon, I discovered much later, is known as Intensive Care Syndrome, where through the stress of surgery, life-support equipment and trauma, patients enter a state of psychosis punctuated by vivid lucid nightmares and, when conscious, can manifest extraordinary and bizarre beliefs. The metaphors embodied in my own experience are clear to me now, but at the time made no sense at all. In my dreams I had really believed I was in this place called Limbo (from the Latin *limbus*, meaning the edge or boundary, in this case of Hell) and that I was condemned never to leave it.

To save my life, I'd had to have a hysterectomy. My uterus had been perforated during the routine scrape to remove the tumour, in what is clinically known as an iatrogenic incident. Instead of being healed by a medical procedure, you are harmed. The perforation had gone through the wall of my womb into a major artery. The pain I had felt coming round from the initial scrape and subsequently was internal bleeding. The growth over my ovary was not cancerous, but a massive blood clot, which during the laparoscopy had been disturbed. In recovery, I had begun to bleed vaginally. The dam having broken and found an exit, there was now nothing to stop me bleeding. If I had haemorrhaged anywhere but the hospital, I would have been dead in less than twenty minutes.

I remember coming round from surgery and hearing my gynaecologist saying that in the Yom Kippur war they had transfused over fifty pints into an Israeli female soldier who had her legs blown off in a shell attack. She had survived. They had squeezed fifty-seven pints of AB+ and ten units of plasma into me, and when I think about what happened, I always remember that Israeli soldier and the horror of what she must have gone through.

On regaining consciousness, I remembered the pact I had made, not with the God of my convent schooling – whom I had long since given up on for being remarkably unhelpful – but with creation, the universe, the love I felt for my life, my children and the world I was lucky enough to have remained in. I had told myself between the bleeds and panic-stricken moments when I thought I was going to die, that if I survived I would somehow change my life. That is what you do when you know you are about to lose everything you love: you make a pact, even while knowing it's a corny thing to do.

I knew I needed to change myself for the better and live a life I truly loved. I couldn't pretend any more. I would try to make a contribution to my world that was meaningful and hopeful. Though I recognised that this wouldn't happen overnight, I was determined that, little by little, I would work through it all and discover a way to express the love I felt for my life and the lives around me. It seemed to me that I had been asked a question I couldn't ignore; the answer lay in me and only me, but I would need help to find it. I couldn't do it by myself because the question had been put to me in terms of loss: the loss of a much-wanted child, the loss of my fertility, the horrible realisation that, still only in my twenties, I was barren, my sense of femininity destroyed. Crucially, however, I was not beaten. My fear of living had come full circle. To make sense of what had happened, I realised I had to grasp a universal truth: that out of destruction comes creation. I finally understood that I had the freedom to choose, no longer at the mercy of my self-doubts, my fear of failure or of having to please other people.

In taking responsibility for myself I was creating the possibility of freedom of choice. I just had to choose wisely for myself from now on. To quote Jean-Paul Sartre once more: '*La vie humaine commence de l'autre côté du désespoir*' (Life begins on the other side of despair). This life-changing event was my entry ticket into the game of life. Now I just needed to create the game I wanted to play. I finally realised what I had to do. I had to choose to take responsibility for myself. It wasn't anyone's fault that my life was the way it was. It was mine and mine alone. If I wanted it to be different, it was up to me. And only me.

## Week Three

### Cognitive

In your journal reflect on your relationship with freedom. Write down any barriers you perceive may be holding you back and then ask yourself, 'Why?' Some impediments may have an external truth, such as a disability or loss; these we cannot change. Yet far more of the blocks that we create for ourselves are internal in origin, and can be overcome by playing with the notions we have about ourselves and creating more constructive ways of thinking.

Here are some phrases that you can use to make powerfully positive reframes of your experience and give yourself freedom to make the changes that you desire in your life.

Practise them as affirmations, meditate on them in your journal, write them on little cards and have them in your wallet, bag or stuck to your mirror. Remember that repetition makes learning easy and will, with practice, change the way you think about yourself and your life.

- Freedom is won through taking risks.
- We are free when we take responsibility for ourselves.
- Desire creates the crucible for change.
- Forget perfect conditions – act now.
- Change is available in each and every moment.
- Embrace radical acceptance to set yourself free from your past.
- I can learn to be who I want to be by being inspired by the best that life has to offer.
- My imagination is my only limit if I am prepared to put the work in.
- I will say 'Yes!' whenever an opportunity arises to learn something new about myself and my life.

Continue to use the thought record to tackle any sticky negative thoughts that continue to obstruct you. Using the thought record every day will by now be having a profound effect on the way you think about yourself. By the end of the third week, as your first twenty-one days draw to a close, you should now be able to maintain a thought record in your head. If you cannot, do not worry, a little more practice will get you there.

**Behavioural**
This week, take some manageable risks. Find a different route to work every day, even if it means getting off a couple of

stops early (you can use this in conjunction with your walking). Start work early, allowing you to leave earlier. Walk your children a different way to school, or cycle to your office rather than using public transport. Mixing it up in this way will show you that you can become more adventurous even in your daily routines. The more fixed and rigid we are habitually, the more fixed and rigid our thinking is prone to be. Make a note in your journal recording how you felt after changing something as simple as eating a different cereal or fruit for breakfast, or having lunch out of the office at least once this week.

Increase your daily walk to twenty minutes. At the weekend, get out into the countryside, or a park. Spend a few hours walking in nature, near water if at all possible. If the weather is fine, take a rug and lie down for a while, observing the sky, the grasses, the bugs and birds; the stiller you become, the more you will be aware of. Know that you are filling yourself with good and nurturing experiences that will increase your emotional and physical wellbeing.

Continue to eat your good-mood foods. While following a serotonin-supporting diet, be careful not to overload on meat – and if you use fish to replace meat, remember to buy from sustainable sources. Consider, too, the amount of alcohol you drink. As well as contributing to ulcers, liver disease, cancer, weight gain, high blood pressure and sexual dysfunction, alcohol contributes significantly to low mood and is often implicated in incidents of self-harm.

The official recommendations for alcohol intake are no more than fourteen units per week for women and twenty-one for men, with at least two alcohol-free days a week. But these recommendations are approximates only; it would probably be more sensible to consider alcohol as a treat, rather than a regular part of your diet. A glass of wine in a bar accounts for about two units, ditto a pint of beer, while a double measure of spirits can count for up to three units. To cut down the amount of alcohol you consume, sip rather than gulp, drink halves instead of pints, have water or soft drinks between alcoholic ones, and wait until your glass is empty before refilling so that you know how much you have really had to drink.

**Emotional**
Identify all the people in your life who make you feel good, relaxed, confident and loved. Commit to spending more time with them. Our friends form a significant part of our support network and are vital to our wellbeing; without them we soon flounder. Bonding with friends releases endorphins in the brain, enhancing mood and boosting the immune system by increasing the amount of immunoglobins and T-Cells in the body (these are the cells that fight infection). Being with friends who make us feel good and with whom we can relax and have fun is essential for our physical health. Laughter reduces blood pressure and increases blood flow, which is good for the heart, eases pain, reduces stress-hormone levels, and alleviates the effects of allergies, including hay fever.

Arrange to meet up with your friends regularly; plan ahead and put these meetings in your diary as part of your reward system. Having future events we can look forward to lifts our mood and keeps us going.

Over the course of week three, plan an activity laden with emotional content. It could be a visit to an art gallery, a cheap opera or theatre ticket, or some other live music or dance event or a powerfully moving movie or DVD. Allow yourself to become fully absorbed in the emotions that arise in you. Observe them, distinguish each one: 'Ah, this is my sadness,' or 'This is my joy' or 'This is my anger'. Notice the colour, depth and resonance of the emotion and then observe it pass through you to be replaced by something else. The idea is not to hang on to the emotions, for this is what we do when we are reacting to them or enacting them. The key is to observe them as they arise, notice them for what they really are and then watch them leave. If you remember that it takes only ninety seconds for an emotion to be triggered, flood through your body and start to dissipate, you will realise that all too often we are hang on to negative emotions for no good reason.

*General reminders at the end of the first three-week cycle*
At this stage your journal should be rich with thought records, snippets of poems, inspiring quotes, pictures, fabrics, leaves or petals, anything in fact that has moved you or helped you connect with your emotional repertoire.

Don't forget to refer back to your change plan and keep working on the goals you have set yourself. Be patient with yourself and don't forget those intrinsic rewards. A relaxing, warm bath (studies show that people who soak regularly in a bath tend to be happier and more relaxed than people who don't), home-made slow as opposed to fast food, a stroll around your neighbourhood, a visit to the countryside, and connecting with valued friends should now be routine weekly activities for you as you develop a more loving relationship with yourself.

## Cognitive Reframe: Future Perfect

If you feel so inclined, spend some time setting down on paper your perfect life, describing where you would like to be in five years' time. Include everything, from the house you want to live in, the person you want to be living with, the children or grandchildren that you want to have – even the little outfits they will be wearing – throw in the car you want, the perfect career, and all those spectacular holidays too. Indulge! Spend a few minutes reading your perfect life out loud to yourself. Really enjoy the fantasy, revel in it, perhaps even share it with someone. Now be really brave and tear the whole lot up into tiny shreds, toss them in the air and let them float to the ground like confetti.

It may seem harsh, to wilfully tear up your dreams, but this exercise is in fact one of the first steps in getting close to reality. Your future simply has not been created yet. None of us know what is really out there for us. But what we do know is that we have potential: potential to be who we really want to be in every moment. A prescriptive list like this doesn't help you to explore yourself and your life. By insisting on the minutiae of dotted i's and crossed t's, we merely close down the unknown number of opportunities available to develop our full potential.

There are no rules you have to follow now; your life doesn't have to be a certain way. You have a beautiful blank page in front of you, and it is yours to do with as you please. This might seem scary at first, like getting rid of all those disappointments on your mobile phone – the ones who never called you back, or just plain let you down. But as soon as you press 'delete', you make space for something else to happen: new numbers come along that are much more promising than the old. As with everything in life, to bring in the new we must sweep out the old. Now we can ask ourselves, 'Where does our real future lie?'

# 4

## Changing Your Life

My plans for life-long distraction disappeared in a deluge of my own blood. Having married and had children so young, I realised that, when my two boys were grown up, I would still be relatively young and would not know what to do with myself. Now, unable to have more children, it dawned on me that I would have to do something else with my life. I had to honour the pact I had made with myself. I had no more excuses – it was time to start making the changes I could so clearly see needed to be made.

But being open to change is not easy. Change requires an act of faith. Faith in ourselves, faith that we will be carried by the support of the world we inhabit, faith that we are choosing a path that is good and nurturing. Until we can become genuinely open to the possibility of change, nothing will change for us. If we stay wedded to the idea that our way is the right and only way, then we will simply continue to do all the things that we have done before. This surely is madness, as Einstein pointed out: to do the same thing over and over and expect a different result.

For things to occur differently, we need to be open to the possibility that there may be other responses, more skilful, more helpful, which will, once we have embraced them, create in us the space that change requires in order to flourish. Maintaining a rigid and self-justifying stance long after it has ceased to yield anything useful, will just keep us feeling stuck and dissatisfied; if we are to move on we must gradually relinquish the need to feel we are always right. The requirement to be 'right' is rooted in our urge for security, however tenuous. Having the courage to step into the unknown, without questioning who is 'right' or 'wrong', frees us to truly explore our lives. We are stepping into the unknown because we have no choice. Taking that first step is not easy because we risk being wrong, which is why so many of us end up staying in the world we know, despite its suffocating limitations.

To live the sort of life I wanted, I had to become open to myself, to the possibility of really being me. Instead of pretending that I was happy, as I had done for so much of my life, I finally admitted to myself that I was actually desperately unhappy, suffocated in a life that didn't make any sense to me. Instead of running away from confronting the truth about myself – that I wasn't living the sort of life that I had imagined for myself – I realised that I needed to make changes, changes that would mean disrupting the safe-but-dull way of life I had adopted in order to avoid taking risks.

To become more open to the possibilities that life might hold, I had to allow myself to dream, something I had always avoided doing, as it had felt too painful to me. All the things I desired – a career that was meaningful, independence, challenging and interesting experiences – felt too remote, too unattainable. I needed to learn to imagine the life I really wanted to live, rather than the life I thought I should live. As Yeats so wisely said, 'In dreams begin responsibility', so finally, through nearly losing my life, I realised that I had to take responsibility for my own happiness. That this was up to me, not other people.

Being open to yourself feels risky, because it means accepting who you really are and then going for what you want regardless, leaving behind old, unhelpful stories about yourself. Being open allows us to tell a new story, one that is constructive, positive and which welcomes the challenges that change inevitably brings to our lives. In my own case, this meant giving up my 'story' that I couldn't change my life and telling myself, instead, that I had nothing to lose by trying to change it.

The first step towards changing my story – which would become integral to changing myself – meant enrolling at my local university and taking a degree in psychology. For some of my patients, telling a different story about themselves has meant no longer remaining identified with their depression or anxiety and instead reconnecting with aspects of their personalities that had become neglected, such as their resilience and resourcefulness, thereby engaging more in the life that surrounds them rather than the 'illness' that has dominated their internal life.

We often feel that if we were just a little more attractive, confident or successful then we would be free to be who we really want to be. This myth is consistently unhelpful as it keeps us trapped, waiting for a future that never arrives because we have created unrealistic conditions for change to take place. For myself, I kept hoping that someone or something would 'rescue me', magically giving me all the things that I wanted without me having to do any of the work to get them. We wait for the perfect conditions to arise, not realising that they never will, as there is no such thing as perfect. Then we wonder why we aren't happier, more open to our experiences and more fulfilled.

We have to choose to be open. In doing so we can start to process what each experience really feels like, and thus begin a truly transformative relationship with ourselves. One of the ways that we can do this is to identify an area of our lives where we feel closed or shutdown. It might be that our career feels stagnant or that we're in a relationship that isn't going anywhere. The first step to change is to ask ourselves some constructive questions and explore our responses.

For example, faced with a feeling that we are under-performing at work, rather than dwelling on what we are doing wrong, we need to open ourselves up to the poss-ibilities: what would we like to bring to our work? What qualities, values and meaning might bring about a change in our relationship with our career? Or, if we feel we're in a relationship that has run aground, instead of dwelling on what has gone wrong, we need to open ourselves up to new possibilities by asking: what would we like to do instead? How do we want to be in relation to our partner – loving, warm, forgiving, tolerant?

Instead of defining ourselves rigidly, conceptualising our-selves with a negative list of what we are not – what we don't do, what we don't like, our failings, anxieties and losses – we can begin to be open to the positives in who we are now, what we care about and what we desire. Desire is important here, because without desire we do not progress. Desire creates a crucible for change. Being open to our desires does not mean we have to chase recklessly every whim or fantasy. If we use desire wisely, it can help us design the life we want to live now.

Imagine for a moment a dream you have cherished, one that perhaps you have wanted so much that you haven't dared think about it for a long time because you fear that you may never achieve it. Now open yourself up to the possibility of realising that dream by thinking about the first small step you could take to get there. If you have wanted to work abroad, for example, but have felt afraid of the upheaval, the challenge, the difficulties involved, imagine for yourself what that first step might be. It could be as simple as learning a new language, telephoning the embassy of the country you are interested in and asking them about their immigration policy or joining an online community for ex-pats and asking questions about what their experience has been like.

Rather than keeping the desire a secret, shrouded by fear of failure, we can open ourselves up to what is possible, even if, in the final analysis, we choose to do something different. By being open in this domain of our lives, we can begin to be open in many others.

If we are not satisfied with our lives we can ask ourselves, what is our motivation? Why do we decide to do the things we do? Can we introduce an alternative perspective that will allow something more natural and authentic to occur? For me, one of the first and most important steps for making this transition from being closed to being open was to stop judging my life and myself. In judgement, I remained trans-fixed by my self-imposed rules, regulations and prejudices.

In judging myself harshly, I couldn't help but project my harsh judgements out into the world and this in turn invited judgement back, thereby compounding and confirming unhelpful negative feelings about myself. When feeling insecure, my capacity to be generous and tolerant is reduced. I know that now, but back then my insecurities just fed on themselves until I became so devoured that I would seek out a target and bite back – only to then feel bad about it, with good reason. Taking care of my self-judgements enables me to retain the capacity to be open to others, whatever may occur, to see them compassionately as I would wish to be seen.

Occupying this place of non-judgement, as best I can, frees me from automatic negative responses and allows me to be more compassionate towards myself and, therefore, my world. As a result, I can see myself and others respectfully, with deeper understanding, acknowledging that we all have a history, a context that informs us and sometimes compels us to do things that perhaps we don't really mean to. It is perhaps here that openness really helps us to be ourselves. For openness demands intimacy and intimacy demands openness. The more intimate we allow ourselves to be, the more open we become and vice versa.

Intimacy requires us to reveal something of ourselves that often we would prefer to remain hidden for fear of judgement. The reality, however, is that if we are prepared to open up, then those around us will be prepared to open up in response. Research consistently shows that the more intimate you can be, the deeper and more meaningful your relationships become. If we are open, we can choose to connect with as many people as we like, and the wider we spread our nets, the more we attract into our lives. Even the shyest of us can deepen our relationships with those we care about by allowing ourselves to risk more with a select group. But we might also allow ourselves to become more open to what is possible in our lives, whatever our personality.

For myself, I learned that if I told someone I felt nervous before doing something new and challenging, their support in response to my honesty about the experience changed the way I related to it and my anxiety diminished as a result. At the same time I formed a bond by revealing something about myself that instead of being shaming in fact brought us both closer in our shared humanity. This simple mechanism allowed me to try many new things that previously I had cut myself off from through fear of failure.

One of the most immediate ways we can do this is simply by saying 'yes' instead of 'no'. So much of our experience gets shut down because we automatically decline or deny something unfamiliar, rather than opening up to its potential. Saying yes may take us to unexpected places, introduce us to new people, new skills, a new job. Rather than playing a cautious hand, trade 'Why?' for 'Why not?' and you might just find that life becomes a much richer and broader experience. Of course, there will always be a need to ask 'Why?' where there are serious consequences to our actions, but we shouldn't use it to protect ourselves from taking manageable risks and dropping our guard.

By resolving not to judge ourselves or our experiences, we can move more fluidly into a world of opportunity, adventure, experimentation and creativity. When we are approached by the world we can welcome it in and observe what arises in us as a result. Saying yes to something new often raises our anxieties, but instead of avoiding our feelings, we can just feel them flow through us, knowing that all feeling states are brief and fleeting. The more permeable we become, the more we can move through life with fluidity rather than having life ricochet off us, deflected by the shields we create to 'protect' us. We can learn from everyone if we choose to, and the more we learn, the more open we will be, as we lose our fear and embrace what is possible.

## Techniques to bring about change

Faced with ever-changing pressures, stressors, demands and expectations, we need a strategy that will help us reframe our experiences and emerge with a more balanced perspective. It's important to ask questions that will help us find our centre and make us feel grounded, rather than ones that will only serve to reinforce the feeling that we've become lost to ourselves.

For example, when a relationship breaks down, if we ask, 'Who am I right now?' the answer will probably involve a fragmented series of negatives: hurt, misunderstandings, broken dreams and disappointments, all of which might lead us to behave in ways that we later regret.

If, on the other hand, we ask ourselves, 'Who do I want to be right now?' it will prompt us to list the qualities and attributes that we aspire to in the face of our distress. We might want to be compassionate, alleviating suffering and showing kindness towards ourselves and our ex. Despite our unhappiness, we might want to be forgiving of any wrongdoing that we or our ex have engaged in, for destructive behaviour is often brought on by the pain of a relationship breaking down. Even though we hurt at our great loss, we might aspire to be magnanimous, accept that we were not the one, accept that they have found another with whom they are happier. We might want to continue to show that we care, that we will always love them for better or worse, because real love is not limited or conditional, it flows despite ourselves because it is pure.

Instead of rubbishing ourselves or telling ourselves negative, unhelpful things because our relationship has failed, we can concentrate on looking after our wounds, making sure we surround ourselves with good friends, people who care about us, people who will be understanding and not let us down. Simply, in the midst of all our hatred, fury, pain and anguish that threatens to victimise us, we can find a kernel of magnanimity which helps us transcend into a good place: a place where we create a good relationship with ourselves and therefore with others.

In asking 'Who do I want to be?' we can focus on identifying the qualities and values that we admire in others so that we are better able to adopt those qualities ourselves. We may, for example, want to feel warmer towards others, more loving and accepting, more forgiving and tolerant, less irritable and egotistical. We might identify people who are at ease with themselves and their world, who are accepting of the petty problems that litter our everyday experience. We might want to emulate those who are cool in a crisis, who don't take out their problems on other people, who are altruistic and put others before themselves.

We can value in our friends their laughter and loyalty,

their ability to have fun regardless of circumstance, their generosity of spirit and their kindness when we are ill or low. We can see the light that shines in their eyes when they talk about their passions and interests, and realise that we too can share that passion and interest and grow closer and more intimate. We can become more curious, ask questions, show concern and interest at what is happening in the lives of those we come into contact with, instead of thinking that everything revolves around us and what we do. And along the way we might just begin to see that everyone feels alone, frightened, vulnerable, hopeless and needy on occasion, and that in sharing these experiences we feel less alone, less frightened, less vulnerable, more hopeful and also see that we all need each other. 'No man is an island,' said John Donne.

'Who do I want to be?' frees us from the navel-gazing of 'Who am I?' It gives us the opportunity to experiment with who we are, to explore possibilities, to make demands on our potential. Instead of seeing ourselves as immutable and unchanging, stuck in a circular argument where we defeat ourselves over and over, we step outside the debate and introduce difference. The difference we are introducing is to begin to see ourselves differently, to begin to acknowledge that we have untapped potential available to us, if only we will invest in it. It is never too late to start an enterprise, it is never too late to learn, it is never too late to begin again. Each moment we are given is a moment in which we are blessed. For it is in each moment that the potential to be who we really want to be arrives unbidden at our door. All we have to do is open the door and welcome it in.

## Week Four

### Cognitive

Using your journal, practise asking yourself skilful questions that can inspire you to continue developing a good relationship with yourself. Try answering these to get you started:

- Who do I care about?
- What do I believe in?
- What do I care about?
- What do I care enough about to want to invest in, emotionally, materially, physically?
- What sort of person do I want to be in relation to conflict?
- What sort of person do I want to be in relation to love?
- How do I want to show my affection and respect for myself?
- How do I want to show my affection and respect for others?
- What qualities are important to me?
- Do I care about truth?
- Do I care about loyalty?
- Do I care about spirituality, politics, charities, animal welfare, ecology?
- If so, which of these issues do I wish to invest in and how?
- Of my personal qualities, which ones matter to me most?
- Are there things about myself I would like to be different, and if so what?
- Can I change these things and if so how?
- If I cannot change these things, can I make the most of what I have and live with what I cannot change?
- What qualities am I looking for in another as a friend, a partner, a lover?
- Can I bring those same qualities to the table myself and if not, why do I expect them in someone else?

- Can I learn from others?
- What can I learn from others that will help me progress to where I want to be?
- What mentors in my life can guide me and teach me?
- What questions do I want guidance with?

Continue with your thought record, noting any sticky negative thoughts and challenging any negative core beliefs that may recur, skewing your thinking. Continue to reflect on your affirmations, adding any that you particularly want to focus on. Remind yourself that you can create new neural networks that are more helpful and constructive with only three weeks of intensive and consistent focus.

## Behavioural

Continue to eat for your wellbeing. Your walk should now be twenty-five minutes long and the pace should be active and revitalising. This weekend, plan a pot-luck picnic with friends and/or family in your local park or woodland. Ask everyone to bring some wellbeing foods and spend a few hours relaxing together. If it rains or is exceptionally cold, ask your friends over to yours. During the week, collect beautiful pebbles or find some other creative way of offering a simple keepsake to your friends that is not about money or materialism.

Breathe in the world 'let' and breathe out the word 'go' when feeling uptight, tense or mired in negativity. Repeat until you feel more settled, it will not take long.

## Emotional

Look at the answers you have given when answering the

questions in the cognitive workshop exercise this week and circle them, using your brightly coloured pens, every time you have used a word that describes an emotion. Then read your answers again, this time focusing on the emotional content of each statement. Observe your feelings as you do so and make a note of anything that surprises or inspires you. If you notice that your emotions are predominantly helpful and nurturing, meditate on your progress so far and consider why things are changing for you. If the emotional content is heavy with negative associations, use the thought record to help you arrive at more balanced perspectives. Don't be afraid to play with your responses; this is not to dismiss your feelings, but to find ways of letting them pass more naturally through you, rather than holding on to them indefinitely.

Whenever the opportunity arises, tell your friends and family how much they mean to you. Do not be ashamed to do this, our lives are too short not to.

## Cognitive Reframe: Rescuers

Many people who had problematic childhoods become 'rescuers' as adults, in an attempt to repair the damage of their earlier experiences. The main way they go about this is by forming romantic attachments with people who in some way appear to need 'fixing'. Rescuers are good people who have an overwhelming need to help others, often at their own expense. Starting a relationship hoping to change someone for the better happens surprisingly often. Rescuers feel that, if they invest exponentially, sublimating more and more of their own needs into loving someone else, they will, in return, be loved back. But no matter how hard we might try, we cannot really change others. Any changes that do come about usually arise because the object of our efforts is serendipitously emotionally available and willing to try something different. Mostly, however, it doesn't happen, because the change crucially has to be in us, not in them. People are emotionally damaged for a reason, and it is for them to find resolution when they are ready.

Sometimes we find ourselves wanting to be transformative in someone else's life, because we do not think we are worthy of the effort in our own life. If this is you, maybe it is time to give up the premise that you have to help someone be worthy of a relationship. Instead, try investing in yourself. After all, are you not worth loving unconditionally? Take a compassionate look at yourself right now. How do you love, nurture and cherish yourself? Is your life all give and no take? Ask yourself why you don't take. What it would be like if you were to value what you need in a relationship for it to work for you.

Next time you are attracted to someone, ask yourself whether you are attracted because they need your help or because they don't. You might find yourself pleasantly surprised by how attractive someone who doesn't need 'rescuing' can be. Confidence, joyfulness, a lightness of heart, not taking yourself too seriously and, most importantly, emotional honesty, are all signs of a healthy ego that is not in need of resuscitation. Now tell yourself that you are worth relating to someone who relates to you with integrity.

# 5

## Embracing Life

When my younger son started primary school, I enrolled myself at the nearest university to my home so that I could drop my children at school, drive to my lectures and be back in time to pick them up. After they were asleep, I would pick up my books and study. Psychology was my passage to freedom, to a new life, not just in terms of the career possibilities it represented, but more importantly to understanding myself and the lives around me.

More than anything I needed to know 'why?' – Why was I the way I was? Why were other people the way they were, and what were these other ways of being? I could see that there were people who seemed serene and able to sustain loving intimate relationships, and I wanted to know how they did it.

It had finally dawned on me during my long convalescence that the way to find out was to study minds and emotions. It wasn't so much that I wanted to be a psychologist; I *needed* to be a psychologist. I began to understand the concept of having a calling. I immersed myself completely in study, convinced I would find solutions to the dilemmas I faced. After a period tussling with whether I wanted to become an academic or a clinical psychologist, working with patients, I finally opted for the latter, giving up a Medical Research Council pre-doctoral fellowship at the Institute of Psychiatry, where I had been researching gender differences in depression. I realised I wanted to work with people more than scientific journals.

Above all, I wanted to learn how to offer something that might help. I wasn't sure yet what form that help would take, but I had an instinct that training to be a clinician would give me the tools I needed. I could also see that being a therapist meant that I could experience therapy every day, and perhaps that was something I needed for myself.

During my time as a researcher at the Institute of Psychiatry, I had been suffering what I thought were migraine auras with increasing regularity. My vision would become obscured with waterfall effects or strange zigzag flashings. Tiny black specks floated across my eyes, but no headache followed. Sometimes the auras would be so powerful that I would have to lie down, or, if driving, pull over until they had passed. I remember working so dizzyingly hard at one point that I thought my brain would explode. In an unusual digression from my thesis on depression I became fascinated with research on strokes (among other things, I learned that golfers were often likely to have a stroke while on the green, and that holding a telephone cradled between your chin and shoulder increased your chance of stroke by cutting off the blood supply to the brain).

Towards the end of my first year of clinical training, I began to experience intense fatigue. I felt weakened, as if slowly unwinding. It got to the point where I would think twice about taking a book to read on the Tube because of the weight of carrying it. I put it down to tiredness because of the stress of training to be a clinical psychologist: placements were demanding; we were expected to carry large caseloads, sit exams, write essays, case histories, and collect data while researching and writing up a doctoral thesis.

Then, one Saturday morning, I was fooling around in the kitchen with the wonderful man I had fallen in love with after my divorce. We were laughing as I complained that I was too tired for such energetic shenanigans. Abruptly, my sight seemed to implode and everything went black. Unable to see and unable to stand, I fell into his arms: confused, neither of us knowing what was happening. I must have blacked out momentarily, sinking into some Moroccan cushions we had strewn about the floor. After about ten minutes, I could see in blurred doubles out of my right eye, but was conscious I could barely use my left. There was a strange darkness where my peripheral vision had been, with odd flashings of kaleidoscopic colour and intermittent glaring brightness where once I could see. I felt very ill. Assuming it must be an intense migraine aura, I thought I should probably lie down for a bit.

I slept for twelve hours, and woke feeling as if an ice-pick was being plunged into my skull; a sensation that did not abate for many hours. Vision in my left eye had not returned. By this time I was beginning to doubt this could be a migraine. I stayed in bed, trying to sleep off the pain, while my partner arranged for me to see my very helpful GP. She wanted me to go to my local hospital to have some neurology tests done immediately, as she thought I had suffered a stroke.

A stroke refers to problems with blood vessels carrying

oxygen to our brain cells. There are two types, ischaemic and hemorrhagic. With the far more common ischaemic stroke, a blood clot travels through an artery until the artery is no longer wide enough for the clot to pass any further. It then gets stuck, blocking the flow of oxygenated blood to the brain cells beyond it. These cells then become traumatised and often do not regenerate.

I wasn't shocked by the diagnosis as I had arrived at much the same conclusion when my vision hadn't returned after two days. After a four-hour wait in A&E, an overly officious junior doctor told me I was wasting her time, and that I merely had a migraine, despite me manifesting four of the six classic symptoms of stroke. I had tingling and numbness in my left arm, was off balance and disorientated, had a painful headache and problems with my eyes, particularly my left eye. I had also experienced a brief period of unconsciousness, when I had blacked out. (The other two main symptoms are: problems with speech or language, and problems with memory.) Just as no two brains are the same, no two strokes are the same, but all strokes are counted as medical emergencies – or at least they should be. The 'follow my finger' eye test I was given was comically inept.

I experimented with being assertive, explaining that I really needed to see a neurologist, as this was more profound than migraine: my vision had not returned and both my GP and I thought I might have suffered a stroke. At this, she marched me to a telephone, rang my GP, remonstrated with her, saying that there was nothing wrong with me and that she should tell me to go home. She then held out the phone for me to listen, as if I was a naughty child, while my embarrassed GP explained that she was sorry but there was nothing she could do and I would have to leave the hospital without a diagnosis.

So began the saga of the ischaemic infarct in my right occipital lobe, which the medical professionals treating me appeared to be in complete denial about. I won't bore you with the details, but suffice to say that over many months of investigation I was told by a succession of specialists that I had MS, two different types of brain tumour, chronic fatigue syndrome – one particularly brilliant diagnosis declared that I clearly 'thought too much' – and that despite only having thirty degrees of vision remaining in my left eye, I was a malingerer, wasting everyone's time.

Early in the investigation of my condition, an endo-crinologist, having ascertained that I wasn't his problem, told me not to bother seeing any more specialists, particularly a cardiologist, as my heart wasn't the issue, judging from my only slightly abnormal arrhythmia. He took great delight in concluding that I was suffering from a psychosomatic manifestation, finding it all the more amusing considering my profession. I sat in restrained silence as he ridiculed my profession, my symptoms and me.

It took over nine months to get an appointment to have a brain scan using the MRI scanner at the Institute of Psych-iatry, where I had been scanned as part of research projects back in the days when I worked there. The scan showed that I had indeed suffered an ischaemic infarct in the right occipital lobe of my brain. The occipital lobes are at the back of the brain and enable vision, each lobe of the right and left brain hemispheres corresponding with the opposite eye. Hence the stroke in my right occipital lobe affected mainly my left eye. As such, I would need to have my heart checked out after all, in case it was implicated in the stroke. Rather as the endocrinologist had done, the cardiologist told me that there was little point in having further tests: many women had an irregular heartbeat and there could be nothing wrong with my heart else it would have been discovered by now. I said nothing, except that I wanted to have the test done anyway.

When my appointment finally came to have my heart investigated, the echocardiogram clearly showed a large hole, called a patent foramen ovale (PFO), between the right and left atrial chambers. The junior doctor who undertook the procedure had to inject me with a saline solution to track the progress of blood that needed oxygenating to see if any of it was leaking between the chambers of my heart. He managed to successively miss the vein and eventually went right through it and out the other side, squirting saline solution and covering me in blood at the same time. Eventually, after much apologising, he located the congenital hole, which hadn't been picked up when I was an infant because it was so large there was no murmur.

Fascinated, I watched the monitor as the saline solution travelled up through my venous return system, which carries deoxygenated blood back to the heart to be pumped into the lungs for oxygenation. The saline exploded through the hole like a stream of champagne bubbles passing from one atrial chamber to the other (blood can flow in either direction through the hole in the septum, the wall between the atrial chambers).

To my untrained eye, the opening looked huge and it was clear, even to me, that I would need surgery to have it closed. At this point the machine rather predictably, given the unwitting ineptitude of my treatment to date, broke down, leaving all my data locked up within. But no one at the hospital bothered to tell me that. Unknowingly, I was waiting for an appointment for surgery that was never going to come.

As I didn't seem to be receiving any constructive treatment, my parents, perplexed that I was ill yet again, kindly arranged for me to be seen by a private cardiologist in Harley Street. Having heard my history, he told me that I needed a PFO closure immediately, given how long it was since I had the original infarct (nearly twelve months had gone by) as I was now at considerable risk of having another, potentially cata-strophic stroke. It is believed that PFO strokes are caused when tiny specks of matter attach themselves to the flappy tissue around the hole, collecting into minute particles, which once detached, enter the bloodstream. Possibly a tiny clot such as this had been loosened from the wall of the hole in my heart and travelled up to my brain. It was also possible that the earlier 'migraines' I had suffered were in fact mini-strokes.

The operation would entail sealing the hole with a titan-ium plug, which would be threaded through my venous system by a catheter into my heart, starting in my groin. Prior to this extraordinary technological advance, I would have had to undergo open-heart surgery: ribs broken, heart removed, plugged and replaced. I was so grateful that I would not have to endure anything so terrifying. Over time, tissue would grow around the titanium device, permanently closing the hole, allowing my heart to function optimally. My risk of having another stroke would then fall back to that of the general population. It sounded like a very good idea to me!

The cardiologist offered me a place at the top of his list privately or I could wait to see if he could squeeze me on to his NHS list. This would be at a different hospital to the one which had so far misdiagnosed my condition for nearly a year, tried to persuade me not to have any more tests and, upon finding that I needed surgery to prevent me from having another stroke, mislaid the data and failed to offer me any follow-up appointments for treatment. I felt truly blessed that my parents had arranged for me to see this doctor and that he had instantly taken my situation seriously and offered me a solution. I couldn't afford the £10,000 it would cost to have the operation privately, as I was still a student studying for my doctorate, so decided to wait out the next few weeks in the hope that a place on the NHS list would come up for me as soon as possible.

In the meantime, he arranged for me to have a trans-oesophageal echocardiogram to take photographs of my heart through my oesophagus. A long, thick, white tube with a camera on the end was pushed down my throat, into my stomach, and rotated to accurately locate the hole. This is a somewhat unnerving experience, often requiring sedation, as the gag reflex is so powerful it can be hard to insert the tube. I lay on the couch focusing on my breathing, relief flooding through me as the camera was whipped out of my throat, lashing snake-like through the air. Again, I was so grateful that something was being done at last. The sense of relief was extraordinary and I suddenly realised the level of stress that had been weighing me down all year; the feeling of not knowing what was wrong with me silently permeating every moment of my day.

As I waited for surgery, I was keenly aware how fortunate

I was: my stroke was relatively minor and I knew I had been through worse in the past. I had been here before and this time I wasn't scared. I had waited this long for treatment: if fate really wanted me, I figured, it would take me whatever. I had learned to respect rather than fear death. This fundamental change in my approach to dying was transformative.

The stroke forced me to slow down. I was very weak: my left arm felt as though it belonged to someone else, flopping feebly at my side; my vision remained significantly impaired and the fatigue I felt before the stroke continued long after it. My brain seemed to fizz and pop persistently, while the area of the brain that had gone bang seemed to cool after the explosion. Life was, once more, trying to tell me something.

I didn't know whether I was suffering from an incurable disease, a brain tumour, or whether I would have another catastrophic stroke. I was no longer able to avoid the reality of death. Why did life keep asking me this horrible question? For the third time, I had to take notice of the one thing I didn't want to fully acknowledge. My life, despite the changes I had made, was still a circle of fear. I was consuming this miraculously saved life of mine, without tasting it; so greedy was I to gobble it all up. My clinical training could not have come at a better time: I really needed to attempt to deal with death, for myself and for my patients, because I knew very well that I was not the only one at this particular party.

As far as we can tell, we are the only species that lives knowing we are going to die. This is as sado-masochistically paradoxical as it gets. There are three stages to dying: the

process of dying, the moment when we pass into unconsciousness and finally, the time after we have died. We don't
need to fear them, we are told, because if we look carefully
at each stage, what is there to fear? Logically that may be the
case, but still I struggle with this thing called dying: I don't
want it, I don't like it and it bothers me. I certainly needed a
game plan to deal with it: how best to finally reconcile that
life means death too?

Reflecting on these stages, I tried to work it out. What
I came up with is not ideal, certainly not brilliant, but it's
what I arrived at. To philosophise about death is, in many
ways, to do it a disservice. Death holds one clear message for
us all: every one of us is working towards our ending, whether
we are conscious of this or not. The more aware we are, the
more we can work towards a good one.

In the process of nearly dying, I worried that I would suffer
pain, and I did. Pain is an inevitable and unavoidable part of
being alive; it is the mechanism through which the body tells
the brain there is trauma that needs acknowledging. If it is not
managed skilfully, our relationship with pain can be such that
we suffer more because we fear it. Knowing we have already
experienced pain, however, helps us to arrive at an understanding that there is no reason we won't also be able to
manage the process of dying. Professor Jon Kabat-Zinn[6] points
out that, even in the midst of our suffering, there is a small
part of us that observes ourselves experiencing the pain and,
as such, feels no pain in bearing witness. This isn't easy to
master; it requires moment-to-moment mindful awareness of
what is occurring. We will come back to this later.

[6] J. Kabat-Zinn, *Full Catastrophe Living* (Piatkus Books, 2001)

If we fear terrible, agonising pain, such as with a cruel terminal illness, we can remember that death becomes a friend to us when we can no longer go on. For me, this was when I felt I could no longer cope with the pain of haemorrhaging. The exhaustion and fear, combined with the agonising clots of blood forced out of my body, left me longing for reprieve: I now understand when someone has had enough and wants their suffering to end. Death offers us an ending to something intolerable that robs us of our dignity and the ability to live our life the way in which we want to.

We might also be afraid of death because we feel we have not realised all our dreams, living with a haunting, nagging doubt that we have achieved nothing. My overcompensation for my near-misses and supposed failures meant that I had pushed myself beyond my limits, as witnessed by the occurrence of the stroke. I had a congenital weakness, yes, but I had not taken enough care of myself. I had ignored the evidence. I had chased the myth of immortality and believed that, if I kept achieving, I could cheat loss. My manic pursuit of my external world had foreclosed on a more fruitful and nurturing adventure: a deep and abiding relationship with my internal world. I was blinded, literally, to what I had been doing to myself.

So I realised something else. Few of us will be lucky enough to have everything we have ever 'wanted' in our lives (it is always humbling to observe that there are millions, globally, who do not even have what they need). Just because this is so, however, doesn't mean we haven't lived a contented life, or a life that we have loved. What matters is focusing on what we care about; acknowledging what we have achieved, what there is yet to achieve, and what is meaningful to us while we are still here.

Material success is no indicator of happiness. After covering our basic needs – where it undeniably makes a significant difference to our sense of wellbeing – an excess of money makes us no happier or more fulfilled. The way in which we measure our lives, if taken from a purely material perspective, would end up being a hollow, desultory affair of merely listing assets.

How much richer we are if we can appreciate the love we share, the people we care about, the places we have been, the thoughts, dreams and imaginings of those around us, the songs we sing, the dances we sway to, the nature we marvel at – the overwhelming beauty of the world around us. How can we not be moved by these things that matter so much more than our job title, our pay cheque, the size of our house or the number of cars we may own? For it is always the person that matters, not the things they possess.

The second stage of dying is when we slip into unconsciousness. For many people, this feels terrifying; at that moment, we think we truly lose control. Yet the reality of the unconscious state means we simply will not be aware of its arrival. When I became unconscious while I was haemorrhaging, I knew nothing at all. All there was, and is when we are unconscious, is nothingness. This nothingness holds no pain, no fear, no torture, no sense of anything – therefore, it does not hurt us.

The experience of becoming unconscious is identical to falling asleep, and falling asleep is a wonderfully benign process of 'relinquishment'. To fall asleep is simply to gently drift away. For all of us, at some point in our all too short lives, we will finally drift away for good, making space for another life to enjoy their time here and embrace it with courage and freedom. Being asleep is one of my favourite experiences: not only entering a whole new dimension through dreams, but also a daily reminder of the gift of life. Asleep, unconscious, like a small death; to awaken a rebirth. Then, of course, there is the time after our death; a time of grief for our loved ones. But for ourselves there will be simply nothing, unless we believe in a life after death, which will have its own comforts.

By embracing the reality of death, we can fill our lives with meaning, because if death is to have a purpose, surely it is to make us aware of the brevity of our existence. Instead of being afraid, we can savour the pleasure of breathing the air, walking in the rain, laughing with those we love, working to make a difference: leaving something good behind. Really appreciating being alive goes a long way to removing the fear of death, because each day lived without a fear of dying is a day lived with an exhilarating love of being alive.

Coming to terms with my mortality, working it out as rationally as is possible for a fundamentally emotional being, freed up valuable energy that I'd been wasting in my neurotic fear of the inevitable. I finally understood that there wasn't anything to fear. It is a simple, yet loaded equation: I am born; therefore I die. Instead of futilely pretending otherwise, I can genuinely invest in living. I just needed some more tools to help me find my way.

The months preceding my stroke were physically exhausting and the months after were difficult in that, as well as recovering from the stroke and heart surgery, I was having to adjust to no longer having normal vision. I still have no peripheral vision on my left side and am aware of a mild loss on my right. This means that being in crowds is quite difficult, and driving at night almost impossible. Being unable to see how the crowd around you is moving, unable to pick up the subtle cues of changes of direction, rather as birds fly together in harmony, made me feel clumsy and awkward. People get very irritated if you make contact with them inadvertently, and I soon learned to keep dead ground to my left as much as possible to avoid brushing against or knocking into anyone.

The greatest loss, however, is never being able to see the person on my left socially. All the vital non-verbal clues of engagement, interest or change of attention are lost on me and I often feel as if I am inadvertently blanking them out. There is always an upside, however. I am constantly being surprised by things that appear mysteriously, looming into my awareness at the very last moment when they are almost touching my face, much to the amusement of my friends and children, who regularly attack my left with bizarre objects to make me jump.

I am also deeply aware and humbled by the ability of those with sight impairment, or any other losses, physical or emotional. Patience has become a friend to me, but most of all, learning patience with myself has made me my own friend. I think the main thing I learned throughout that very odd year of my life was to take things one day at a time. In coming to terms with my own impermanence, my own unimportance in the scheme of things, waking to find a new day ahead took on a new and significant aura.

During this period, my clinical training brought me in contact with a new type of cognitive therapy that synthesised

the best of Western cognitive science with Eastern philosophy. This therapy, known as Mindfulness Based Cognitive
Therapy (MBCT), had been pioneered in the United States
by Jon Kabat-Zinn, mentioned earlier, who had become an
inspiring hero to me. These ideas of mindfulness and living
in the moment resonated with my own experience so mean-
ingfully that I started to incorporate them into my work,
particularly when it came to using compassion as way
of alleviating destructive negative thinking and as a means
to value and care for yourself, building self-esteem and
confidence.

Being in the moment is very much a right-brain activity;
the left is more concerned with sequencing data, making
judgements and analysing sensory input. Right-brain activity
is more about the big picture, a sense of the whole and a
feeling of connectedness with each other and the universe.
Imagine the head (left brain) ruling the heart (right brain)
and the conflicts that arise in all of us as a result, or our
thoughts (left brain) dominating our feelings (right brain).
Our internal critic is located in the language centres of the
left brain, creating stories about ourselves that can be negative and hostile, our right brain is where we find our compassionate self that does not want to condemn or fragment,
creating instead a sense of unity and serenity.

Serendipitously, mindfulness had fallen into my life at just
the right time. Dr Jill Bolte Taylor,[7] a renowned brain scientist
and inspirational survivor of a massive haemorrhagic stroke,
locates deep inner peace and loving compassion in the right
brain. It is the right brain that becomes activated during

---

[7] J. Bolte Taylor, *My Stroke of Insight* (Viking, 2006)

meditation with a concomitant quieting of the noisy, chattering left brain. To me, MBCT helps the connected, compassionate, 'at oneness' of the right brain make peace with the judging, critical, story-telling left brain. I adopted its principles and let them guide me through the long period of waiting for a diagnosis and steering a way through the many mis-diagnoses. To me, living mindfully in the moment is not easy; it is a skill that requires revisiting and refining if it is to stay useful. It does, however, provide much solace and reassurance in its central message that everything changes; which when you are going through difficult times is just what you need to hear.

## Week Five

### Cognitive

Continue to hone your reframing skills by checking in with yourself on a daily basis at the start and end of the day, clearing any negative thought processes using your thought record. Revisit any thought records where you became stuck and see if you can play with the thoughts until they become less rigid and uncompromising. Remember that your left brain will want to create 'stories' about your experiences, often packed with unhelpful judgements that may be contributing to any feelings of low mood or anxiety. By now, I hope that you will have discovered for yourself that our emotions are not the problem; it is what we do with them that matters.

Often we are not aware that the stories we tell about ourselves are infused with misplaced and confusing emotions that usually cover up the vulnerable inner selves that we are desperately trying to protect. The more we are able to observe that our vulnerability can be taken care of with loving compassion, the less we will need to defend against our very human feelings of uncertainty, anger, sadness and helplessness by covering our tracks with stories about ourselves that serve no purpose other than to keep us stuck.

Begin to observe the stories that your mind creates with healthy scepticism. Staying attached to the negative stories you tell about yourself does not help you to progress. If you have a particular story that you are prone to repeating, experiment with telling it a different way. The more you can generate a fluid way of relating to yourself, the less your unhelpful stories will transfix you.

Try writing an old negative story in your journal and then read it to yourself out loud. The first time you read it you will probably feel distress, maybe even cry. This is fine and as it should be. Continue to read it aloud, over and over, until you no longer feel anything as you read. When you have reached this point, you will begin to see that this is a story that you tell about yourself, which keeps you locked into a way of relating to yourself that is rigid. The fewer misplaced emotions you attach to your old story, the freer you will become to leave it where it belongs, in the past. In this way you will liberate your present and, therefore, the potential in your future to view yourself in a different way. It is time to tell a new story about yourself, one that is full of hope, inspiration and courage. Now write that story. Do not overanalyse at this stage how you are going to achieve this new narrative about your life, just write down how you want it to look and feel.

## Behavioural

Continue to eat your wellbeing diet. I would urge you to refrain from all caffeine, sugary carbonated drinks and highly processed foods. Your walk should now be a brisk thirty minutes at least five days a week, and if you enjoy swimming add some pool time into your programme. Swimming is soothing and cleansing and has the advantage of being non-weight-bearing, so very good for tired joints. It is the closest we get to floating in space. It is marvellously meditative, just as walking is, and if you are fortunate to have access to a pool where you can steam or sauna afterwards you will further help detox your body. Your body will by now be feeling stronger, healthier and more balanced.

Buy a guided meditation CD that includes a bodyscan meditation in preparation for next week's mindfulness work. A bodyscan meditation is a systematic, progressive meditation that connects you with your breath to your entire body. You can order these securely from www.mind-fulnesstapes.com. The advantage of a guided meditation is that you do not need to worry if you are doing it 'right'.

Learning to relax is a much underestimated art form. Most people do not know how to do it properly and wonder why they constantly feel stressed. Learning how to relax systematically is one of the most nurturing things you can do for your mind and your body. Be open to the experience and do not judge yourself while practising. The more you practise a bodyscan meditation, the more you will be able to manage distress, whether physical or emotional.

## Emotional

Review the story work that you have already done in your journal by comparing your old story with your new one. Note any changes in emotional content between the stories; perhaps highlighting key words with your coloured pens. Explore how you feel about yourself when you compare these two different ways of perceiving yourself. Particularly look out for any feelings of hope, nurturance, growth and development in your new story. These are the feelings that will propel you closer to who you really want to be in life. This work is preparation for the circle exercise found in Chapter 9 – a warm-up, if you like – in which you will push yourself beyond the confined boundaries of your current thinking into a world where you dare to be yourself.

As you unravel your thinking, you will notice a spaciousness where once there was clutter and a stillness where once there was agitation. Enhance these feelings of emerging serenity with a daily symbolic act of compassion. These acts do not have to be grand in scale. A helping hand to a colleague, lifting something heavy for someone weaker or smaller than yourself, giving directions to a stranger cheerfully and with patience, offering up your seat to someone who needs it more than you . . . All of these gestures will help you centre yourself by connecting you to the reality that we are not the centre of the universe. The many worries that preoccupy us are usually relatively insignificant when observing the worlds that many less fortunate than ourselves occupy.

## Cognitive Reframe: Bear Witness

Many years ago, I was lucky enough to spend a weekend with Al Pesso (www.pbsp.com), a dance and movement educator, who discovered that many of his students appeared to have parts of their bodies 'locked', and when they processed certain emotional experiences they became unlocked, able to move freely, with expression. Science is beginning to explore the idea that we carry emotions in our bodies, and that our bodies have a memory for events, which is why anniversaries of trauma or loss can catch us unexpectedly, leaving us feeling destabilised, without realising why. Once we notice what the date is, we then process that we are caught up in a memory of something that has left such a deep impression on us that our bodies are aware of it before our minds have caught up. More evidence that the Cartesian split of mind and body has been nothing but unhelpful in both medicine and psychology for hundreds of years.

Pesso's method is simple but powerful. First, position yourself in the room, just sit and ground yourself with a few breaths until you feel settled in yourself. Now imagine those closest to you – this can be anyone who is meaningful to you – and in your mind's eye, place them in the room. Notice where they are in relation to you and which positions they have adopted. Are they touching you, holding you or supporting you? Are they close to you or far away, perhaps at a distance but still a presence that you value?

Then imagine the parent, relative, friend or caregiver with whom you want to arrive at a resolution. Now in your mind place them in the room. Again, notice where they are in relation to you. Are they close or far away? Ask yourself why you have placed them where they are. If they are far away, is that to help you feel safe? To create distance? Or because you do not know how to approach them yourself? Do not judge yourself or them, just acknowledge where they are and why.

Now bear witness to your experience. Try and adopt a 'third position'; one where you can observe yourself observing what has happened. This witness is compassionate, it does not judge and it is not seeking anything, it just wants to understand what happened to you and why. Once your witness has heard everything you have to say, turn your attention to the person you want to arrive at an understanding with. Begin to populate their world with those people and events which are important to them; their relationships, their losses, their hopes and their dreams. Let your witness observe you doing this, again without judgement, just watching as you begin to create a picture of the life of the person with whom you have an issue.

You will probably start to feel empathy for this person as you observe their life, as you understand it, gradually unfold. When I did this exercise, I realised that the person I had an issue with was lonely, unhappy and unfulfilled. It then occurred to me that they had not meant to be hurtful or cruel, because they appeared to me to be very damaged by their own losses and the problems they had faced in their own relationships, which had left them feeling unlovable and lost. In this way, I began to empathise with them, and although I could acknowledge the effect their behaviour had on me, I could also see that there were reasons why they had behaved this way – reasons which had nothing to do with me. By bearing witness to my own truth and to theirs, as best as I could understand it, I could see that there was no reason for me to continue to feel angry and upset with them.

Bearing witness is not to condone or collude with what went wrong, but to give us some space in which to understand why things might have gone wrong and, in so doing, move a little closer to something reparative and healing. This might simply be an acknowledgement and a letting go, or it could propel us into making steps to re-engage with that person and talk things through, if they are open to such an idea. Whatever the steps you take might be, the point of this exercise is not to try to fix the past, but to understand it and yourself with greater clarity and compassion. The clearer we can be with ourselves, the clearer we can be with others, and that makes things better for everyone in the long term.

# 6

## Learning to Live in the Moment

You may well have heard of mindfulness because it has been around for thousands of years. Although for me it was an epiphany, for others it is simply a way of life. You may also know that it is an Eastern concept, derived from Buddhist practice, about living in the moment. Some explanations of mindfulness can appear intimidating, making us feel that somehow we have to go through extended periods of meditation in order to empty our minds of troubling thoughts – and that seems impossibly time-consuming, given our busy lives. Moreover, how can we empty our minds of anything, let alone troubling thoughts? Yet the exciting reality is that mindfulness is available to us at any time, anywhere and in whatever emotional state we happen to be in, because mindfulness is about being really aware of, and present to, what is happening to us right now, in this very moment.

To give you an example, while you are reading this book, has your mind wandered off? Have you been thinking, 'What am I going to cook for dinner/do at the weekend/pack for my holiday?' The mind tends to do this. Our concentration unravels as our thoughts grab on to the many pressing worries and distractions that are milling about in our heads.

So bringing our attention back to what is taking place right now is mindfulness in action. We don't have to worry about becoming 'enlightened' – which instantly makes us feel inadequate, suggesting as it does, that we are the opposite: unenlightened. The beauty of mindfulness is that it does not demand anything of us. It is just there, waiting patiently for us to, as they say appositely in Northern Ireland, 'catch ourselves on'.

For some of us the notion of living in the present moment is a highly desirable goal. We know it makes sense, but how do we achieve it? Add to this the misconceptions regarding what living in the moment means, and it all becomes rather confusing. Does it imply we have no concern for the future? Does it suggest that the past is irrelevant, or that we must forget about our goals and dreams and just accept whatever fate throws at us? The answer to these sensible and inquiring questions is, somewhat reassuringly, 'No'. To live in the present does not mean you have to forget the past or future, just as you do not have to give up your goals or just passively consent to anything that comes your way.

Living in the moment is about learning to let go of attachment or aversion to our past experiences and to stop projecting those attachments or aversions into our future. It is about creating and defining our long-term goals and allowing ourselves to work actively in the present for them, rather than anxiously worrying about how we are going to achieve them, or imagining that what has happened in the past to sabotage them will inevitably happen again.

Living in the moment enables us to engage with our present experience without judgement, without an assumption that it is going to be more of the same old thing. Living in the moment crucially allows us to start again, time after time, moment by moment. It is also about acknowledging the reality of our experience, rather than denying, repressing or avoiding the accompanying thoughts and emotions. It frees us to accept that these thoughts and feelings are part of our human experience and we can, in the next moment, choose more skilfully and do something that will create a difference for us right now.

Mindfulness is about being in the moment in a very particular way, without judgement. This isn't easy, because the place our thoughts most often wander off to is a place of judgement. One moment you are greeting your friend, pleased to see her, full of warm feelings. The next you are thinking, 'Are those wrinkles? Oh, but my wrinkles are awful. I don't like her dress, but her new bag is amazing. Why can I never find a cool bag? Maybe I haven't got the eye for it. This bar is so noisy. Oh, he's dishy, bet he wouldn't fancy me ...!' And of course, we are also judging ourselves. We become our own worst critics. Our internal dialogue can be full of those harsh, punishing, unrelenting criticisms that bring us down and make us feel worthless.

We might well ask, why do we think like this? Well, in part, we are taught from very early in life to categorise things as either good/bad or right/wrong, so we learn habitually to label all our experiences in this way, including our thoughts and emotions. Being able to judge is a useful skill, one we need for many aspects of our lives. If left unchallenged, however, it can become dominating; unhelpfully permeating all our thoughts and feelings, keeping us at a distance from directly experiencing the moment we are in. For example, have you ever been really excited about going away on holiday, wishing your time away until you can get to your destination, only to find that once you are there you spend all your time wishing your holiday would go on forever and dreading the thought of going back home? It is clear that this sort of thinking profoundly interferes with our ability to enjoy fully the time we have now.

This all seems quite logical, but how do we achieve the seemingly impossible state of being aware in – and of – the present moment? One thing that can really help is to remember that our minds are going to wander and that is just fine. Being 'present moment aware' is not about having an empty mind or a mind free of negative thoughts. Our minds are always going to be alive with thoughts, for consciousness is designed to generate thought after thought. Our first task, therefore, is to understand that while attempting to be in the moment, our monkey minds will want to spring off tangentially, leaping from metaphorical bough to bough. This is normal. All we have to do is be aware that our minds have become unfocused and bring ourselves back to our task, whatever it might be.

A simple way to access this experience is to choose to do one simple thing mindfully every day; something routine and uncomplicated like cleaning your teeth or brushing your hair. Focus all your attention on the task and experience it as fully as you can, using all your senses. Notice what the experience feels like, what arises in you as you perform it, what thoughts and feelings occur to you. Remind yourself that you are not judging how you are doing it – there is no right or wrong way – there is just your mindful attention to the process. If your mind wanders, simply note this and return to the task. You might want to label the thoughts if you recognise them: 'Ah, this is my worry,' or 'This is my sadness.' You might also notice how easy it is to become overly identified with these distracting thoughts and how they take you away from being present.

Developing the skill of mindfulness can subtly change the way we think by enabling us to engage more fully with all our senses, enriching our day-to-day experiences. Practising mindfulness can also help take the pain out of challenging events that might otherwise feel overwhelming, and transform ordinary events into life-enhancing experiences.

Here are five key skills, with thanks to Jon Kabat-Zinn, which we can learn in order to generate a more open, accepting, tolerant and fresh way of relating to ourselves and our lives.

**SKILL 1** – *In the moment without judgement*
Allow yourself 5–10 minutes to practise this skill, slow everything down, your movements and the time you take with each of your senses.

Take a raisin and hold it in your hand. Slowly examine it as if you have never seen anything like it before. Hold it up to the light and carefully observe its texture, shape and colour. Look at this raisin as if you have just arrived from another world and you are completely fresh to it.

Take it to your ear and roll it between your fingers. Does it make a noise? Now smell it. How does it smell? When you have finished exploring it with your sense of touch and vision, take it towards your mouth. Notice how your hand knows exactly where to place it. Become aware of what happens inside your mouth as it approaches.

Observe your thoughts. They might be, 'I don't like these!'

or 'Why am I doing this? I feel self-conscious' or 'I wonder if it will taste as sweet as it looks?' Acknowledge your thoughts as they arise and then let them pass, returning your attention to the raisin.

Next, place it inside your mouth. Notice how your hand and arm know exactly where to put it and how your mouth opens to receive it. Roll it around, exploring its texture with your tongue, without chewing it. Press it against the roof of your mouth and notice the feel of its resistance. Then when you are ready, very consciously take a gentle bite down on to it, noticing the flavour it releases and how it changes in consistency. Chew it slowly, experiencing the process, the movement of your jaw, the meeting of upper and lower teeth. When you feel ready to swallow, again very consciously, notice what happens as you begin to swallow, how the raisin arrives at the back of the throat, how it travels down towards your stomach.

When you finish this exercise, notice how you feel, what sensations, thoughts and experiences you have observed. Ask yourself how free of judgement were you? Perhaps you noticed how often your mind flitted to a comparative, critical or assuming thought, before returning to the task. You may have felt silly, thought the exercise was trivial and pointless, or you may have felt self-conscious or cynical. All these thoughts are just fine; noticing them as they arise in you is mindfulness in action. Perhaps you became so absorbed in what you were doing that you hardly noticed your thinking at all, fully engaging with all your senses. Whatever your thoughts were, remember that there is no right or wrong way of doing this. Being aware of your experience, whatever form it takes, is what is important here.

We can extend this exercise simply by choosing to do one additional thing mindfully every day. Shower mindfully; this can be a revelation as you begin to appreciate fully your body as you wash it with complete focus. At first it might be difficult to do so without judgement, as we are so used to judging our bodies negatively. Remember, if censure comes in, observe it, know it for what it really is – merely a judgemental thought – and let it pass, returning to the task.

Clean your teeth mindfully, drive the car mindfully, drink your coffee or peel the potatoes with your full attention and notice what happens to you when you do so. The more aware you become, the less you are likely to drift into automatic pilot, where we do things mindlessly. Research shows that the more mindfully engaged we are with our lives, the less at the mercy of negative thoughts we become.

**SKILL 2** – *Breathing space*
Another way we can bring ourselves back to the moment is to use our breath to guide us. This skill can alleviate feelings of stress, anxiety and low mood, because it gets us back in touch with that which is truly important: the present. All too often, our negative moods are brought on by mourning the past or worrying about the future. This exercise reminds us that we cannot change the past and we cannot predict the future, but we can notice what is happening around us right now.

Sitting or standing, eyes open or shut, take a few minutes just to breathe. Ideally, inhale through your nose and exhale through your mouth. Some people find this surprisingly hard to manage, and if this is true for you, just breathe through your nose. Once again, you may notice thoughts arising as you breathe, thoughts about what you have to do next, or about things that have already happened. The thoughts might be pleasant or unpleasant, but whatever form they take, just note these thoughts as 'mental events' and let them pass by.

You might also notice sensations in your body, feelings of tension or even pain. Again, allow yourself to acknowledge these sensations, accepting that this is the way you feel right now, without trying to change anything. Then see if you can let the sensations go, just as you did with your thoughts. Turn your attention back to your breath, focusing on how your belly rises and falls, each breath a moment, each moment a breath. Listen to your breath and become aware of the sensations of breathing, the coolness of the in-breath as you draw it down into your body, its warmth as it leaves you.

If you find it hard to breathe in through your nose and out through your mouth, notice how this makes you feel. Don't put yourself under unnecessary pressure to 'get it right': you are not trying to control your breath; the task is just to become conscious of the breath that is unique to you. Breathing mindfully in this way grounds us, allowing us to acknowledge our experience, whatever it might be, without judgement, without feeling we have to fix anything.

SKILL 3 – *Thoughts are not facts*
We become so attached to our thoughts that we often start to believe that everything we think is real. We forget to challenge this misconception with this fundamental truth: thoughts are simply 'mental events', one replaced by another, over and over again. Thoughts are not facts

and most importantly, they do not dictate who we are. Never forget:

*We are not our thoughts.*

To make yourself aware of how frequently we believe our thoughts to be true, observe your thinking for a few moments several times a day. Useful questions to ask yourself might be, 'Is this a thought about the past or the future? Am I confusing this thought with a fact? Am I judging myself?'

The more we become aware that our thoughts will keep on rolling in, like clouds in the sky, one replaced by another, the more we see that they are not 'real'. Our thoughts are the epiphenomena of chemical brain activity; the product of electrical impulses, firing thousands of times a second. How then can we be our thoughts?

You will also start to notice that some are negatively critical while others are openly optimistic and hopeful. By getting to know how you really think, you can then choose to focus on which thoughts are most helpful to you, while letting go of the ones that aren't. This is vitally important when identifying and reframing automatic, negative thinking.

**SKILL 4** – *Capture both pleasant and unpleasant experiences*
All too often we do not allow ourselves to appreciate the moment, because our mind has already abandoned it to think about the next thing. Events that make us feel good are forgotten almost instantly, so when times are hard we have nothing to fall back on. Research confirms what we already know, that our judging mind classifies events as pleasant, unpleasant or neutral. It is at this pivotal moment of judgement that we determine our reaction. If we are

stumbling about on automatic pilot, not only are we going to miss out on important life-affirming events, but we might also classify them as unpleasant, when this isn't the case.

Capturing pleasant experiences by writing down in our journal events that have happened during the day, however small and seemingly insignificant, orientates us to the reality that, however bad things might seem, there are always tiny moments of reprieve. We see that good things can and do occur around us, whatever our circumstances. Noting down these moments means that they are not lost to us. We can record and refer back to them if we are having a particularly tough time, reminding us that there are resources out there that bring us happiness. When we write down these pleasurable events – the sound of birdsong, a great cup of tea, the smell of roses – we can also capture what it feels like to experience them, noticing the quality of the sensations and where we feel them in our body. In this way we start to appreciate how our bodies take in sensory experiences. We become more open to the pleasure our senses can afford us and less reliant on our thinking, which often fails to acknowledge the good things in life, distracted as our mind is by so many concerns. By actively noting pleasure, we also develop a creative dialogue with ourselves that incorporates our thoughts, feelings and physical sensations, storing up a reservoir of wellbeing that we can tap into at any time.

It is just as important to notice what feels unpleasant to you, where you feel it – in your muscles as tension, or in your stomach as nausea or perhaps a palpitating heart or an increasing sense of agitation – and your reaction to the experience. Whether you catastrophise the row you had with your partner, getting cross with your child or missing a deadline as a disaster, unbearable and to be avoided at all costs; or whether you are able to see that this experience, just as a pleasant one, is transient, passing through you like a wave, intense one moment, gone the next.

The less we are on automatic pilot – the more in touch we are with what is really arising in us moment to moment – the more in control of our thoughts and feelings we can be. We do not need to fear what feels unpleasant to us: knowing, understanding and taking care of these experiences is what is helpful.

### SKILL 5 – *Mindfully create your day*

We all know by now that our thoughts affect our feelings. Tumbling out of bed on the alarm, rushing off to work without pausing for breakfast, launching yourself straight into tasks without prioritising, can leave you feeling mangled before you have even got to lunchtime. Instead, each morning when you wake up, however busy you are, give yourself time to lie still, even if it is for just a few seconds. Use the breathing space to ground you in the moment.

Actively visualise the day you desire and the qualities you wish to bring to it, such as serenity, energy, love or patience. Mindfully engaging with your thoughts in this way can produce long-term positive effects in wellbeing as you establish the neural networks that counter-balance negative thinking, while promoting the likelihood of engaging with the positive things that you have visualised and want to experience during your day.

The Mindfulness Based Stress Reduction course pioneered by Jon Kabat-Zinn at the University of Massachusetts found that sixty per cent of people suffering from anxiety and stress-related disorders benefited from a daily mindfulness practice. They include a bodyscan meditation, which guides you in systemically breathing into each part of your body, identifying the different sensations, experiences and thoughts you have as you cultivate your awareness.

Too often we live inside our heads, forgetting that our senses are there to help us explore the world outside our minds. The more we live in our senses, the more we are connected to reality. The more we are connected to reality, the more we are in touch with what is possible in our lives.

Mindfulness allows us to become more aware, and less at the mercy of automatic thinking that can leave us vulnerable to negative thoughts and feelings, lowering our mood and motivation. Many people find the bodyscan relaxing, but that is not the purpose of it, although it can be a welcome outcome of practising the meditation. What is important is that you approach the meditation with openness to the experience, observing the sensations that arise in you without judgement, just noting them and letting them go.

Learning how to meditate can seem difficult. Without guidance we can feel that we should be 'doing it right' rather than being with our experience, whatever that may be. As such, all the meditations are guided, which means you will be instructed what to do throughout the meditation, so that you do not feel alone in your practice.

The more we practise, the more we benefit. Research[8] shows that people who regularly meditate have lower levels of stress hormones in their blood, have calmer brain activity and lower blood pressure. They are less anxious and they often

[8] http://www.anandapaloalto.org/joy/BenefitsOfMeditation.html for example.

find that their mood lifts as a result of their practice. There are many advantages to our health and wellbeing in meditating, but perhaps the most important one is simply taking time for yourself, to centre yourself in your day, preparing yourself to live in each and every moment.

Developing the skill of mindfulness enhances our engagement with all aspects of our lives. It creates freedom to describe ourselves without judgement and in so doing we can tell a different story about ourselves, one that is compassionate, authentic and present to the most important time in our life, which is and always will be, this very moment.

## Week Six

### Cognitive

You are now at the end of the second of the three-week workshop cycles and your journal will be packed full of exercises, observations and inspirations. Well done for getting this far! If you have become adept at cognitive restructuring in your head, jot down any insights you have discovered in your journal over the next week, such as triggers for downward mood spirals or pet negative automatic thoughts that require repeated exposure to this method in order to weaken the neural net and replace them with more nurturing and gentle 'self-soothing' thoughts. At the end of this week reflect on your progress so far; your mind should be becoming increasingly uncluttered and unworried, and your thinking less judgemental, more fluid and gentle.

This week, begin to capture both pleasant and unpleasant events in your journal. Write down three pleasant and three unpleasant events and don't forget to acknowledge how you felt on each occasion. If the unpleasant event continues to bother you, use a thought record to reframe your experience, not forgetting to bring your compassionate right brain in to help you.

Additionally, practise Skill 3, 'Thoughts are not facts', whenever you have a disturbing, distressing or critical thought.

## Behavioural

Practise Skill 1, 'In the moment without judgement' every day this week. Choose one routine activity, such as washing a plate, brushing your teeth or hair, or washing your hands, and bring your mindful awareness to the task. It is important to choose something that you do every day, as this will help you discover whether you remember to bring mindfulness to the task and then what it is like when you do. Note down any observations in your journal. You will find that the experience is never the same twice, which is a useful reminder that everything changes, even the way you wash your hands!

Additionally, practise Skill 2, the breathing space, three times a day. Try to find a set time to practise, such as when you wake up, once at lunchtime and once in the evening, perhaps before you go to sleep (many people find this a relaxing way of getting off to sleep, although this is not its purpose). The more you practise this skill, the more you will benefit from its restorative powers. Don't forget to use the breathing space during the day to help you cope with any pressures that may arise.

Continue to exercise and eat for your wellbeing. Seriously consider reducing your meat intake to a minimum; the less meat you eat the faster your metabolism will become, which will free up valuable energy. Intensively farmed meat is pumped with hormones and is low in nutrients: it is bad for our health, our environment and for the animals subjected to its cruel practices. Meat should be a treat rather than a staple; buy free range and preferably organic to benefit from its higher yield in tryptophan.

You may now want to consider yoga, the benefits of which cannot be overemphasised in balancing mind and body. Yoga can alleviate or prevent back and shoulder pain, asthma and headaches, and reduces anxiety, low mood and stress. The British Wheel of Yoga (www.bwy.org.uk) will direct you to your nearest class.

### Emotional

Every morning this week, before you get out of bed, pause for a moment (perhaps after breathing mindfully) and create your intentions for the day. Be spontaneous; do not judge yourself for what you want to bring to your day. If your mind darts to negative responses, do not react hastily, instead reflect and centre yourself with your breathing. Your intentions can be as simple as having fun, or as profound as wanting to make a difference. Whatever they are, bring your attention to them for a few moments, feel them expand in your awareness and check in with them throughout the day. You may be surprised at just how synchronistically your day pans out after creating it in your mind's eye!

### Cognitive Reframe: Half-Smiling Exercise

On your way to work, on the school run, or going to do some shopping, half-smile. The longer you leave the half-smile in place, the more you will convince your brain that you are feeling happy. The brain responds to physical sensations cued by muscular contractions, and will produce the hormones that relate to the physical cue automatically. If you are smiling, the brain thinks you are happy and the hypothalamus (the part of your brain that produces the chemical messengers that correlate with mood) will respond accordingly, releasing endorphins. The half-smiling exercise can fool your brain into thinking that you are relaxed and happy because you look relaxed and happy. Other people will also perceive you as relaxed and happy, and will interact with you accordingly, reinforcing the feel-good vibe. It is in these tiny but important moments of connection that we begin to feel whole again. At some point you will suddenly feel the way you look: relaxed and happy. Try it, it's amazing how effective it is, impacting immediately on you and your world.

## Cognitive Reframe: How to Reconnect with Your Experience

Many people feel dead inside, living from one fear to another, unable to connect with themselves or their lives. If you are one of these people, ask yourself what killed off your real feelings? Possibly something traumatic happened that has left you empty and hollowed out. Instead of a passion for life coursing through your veins, perhaps you feel a barren wilderness of confusion and regret. The first step that you might want to take to come alive again emotionally is to reconnect with your authentic experience. By this I mean, instead of denying your feelings – be they fear, regret, joy or love – begin to embrace them. They are a part of you and they are desperate for expression. The way we can begin this process is to stop living in our heads and start living in our experiences, which can often be painful.

Often our thinking traps us in an unreal world, a world where we rationalise our genuine feelings away, where the meaning we allow ourselves to make about our lives is based on 'shoulds' and 'oughts' and 'if onlys'. To escape the tyranny of such rigid thinking we can experiment with living through the richness that our senses can describe. A richness found in the quality of light and sound, of taste, touch and scent. Allow yourself to explore the real world you inhabit, not the one in your head. Take time over the little things that sustain us – the quiet sunset, the song of the blackbird, the smell of fresh-cut roses, the touch of skin on skin – fill yourself up with the good things that are freely available to us. Then perhaps ask yourself some questions, skilful questions, about the way you want to live now.

Whatever it is that cut you dead all those years ago, let it go now. It does not help you, it keeps you trapped, fearful of being you, fearful of making emotional contact. Who you want to be right now is what counts. What sort of a husband and father, daughter or sister, do you really want to be? Instead of wasting time on bitter regret, give yourself permission to start being that person right now. It won't be easy, you will have become habituated to suppressing your feelings, so experiment with yourself, surprise yourself and, in doing so, surprise those you care about.

Whatever it is you want to do, do it now – it is never too late to start again. Being in the world is infinitely more important than doing. Who we are being is what counts, not what we have. Explore what it is you value and where you think you could make a difference, however small, and take it from there. Nurture your dreams: the seeds you plant now in the flowerbed that is your imagination will germinate and grow. But also cherish the world of your senses, for it is here that we can connect with our experience and through this connection we can set our emotions free.

# 7

## Confidence and Resilience

As I lay on my sofa resting, I contemplated my hilarious misfortune with health. Yes, my body was covered in scars, various internal organs were missing, titanium plugged up my heart and I was mostly blind in one eye, but there was no doubt: I was a survivor. Despite feeling physically weak, mentally, I felt strong.

I was acutely aware of my gratitude that I was alive. Grateful to all those people who dedicate themselves to healing others; understanding that they couldn't always get things right, but when they did, they saved lives and, once again, my life had been saved. I never consciously harboured resentment towards the medical profession for the iatrogenic injuries, the mis-diagnoses or the unskilful communications. Now, more than ever, I felt nothing but compassion for the demands my illnesses had made on those who were trying to help me. Many times, things had gone wrong, but things had also gone miraculously right and I was alive to prove it; that was what mattered, more than anything else.

From that sense of strength, understanding and gratitude, I began to see that, through facing life's challenges, I was able to comment on my own experience with my self-esteem intact. I began to truly appreciate that, if I did not unfairly judge others – if I could try and see the best in everyone I connected with – then I had no fear of being judged by them. I finally understood that unfair judgement says more about the judger than it does about those being judged. Until someone has lived your life, who are they to judge you? Until someone has experienced your losses or accepted what is true for you with compassion, who are they to condemn you? But most importantly, I had stopped unfairly judging myself, because I now realised it was ultimately my own ruthless self-criticism that was holding me back.

With these realisations grew a nascent sense of confidence, at first quiet and reticent, but increasingly assured; reinforced by the knowledge that even if I do not live my life perfectly, I fully appreciate that perfection does not exist. Even if I make mistakes, they are my mistakes and no one else's. Even if I mess up spectacularly, I can pick myself up again and again and again. Because I can, because I want to, because I care.

This discovery, that by caring enough to take risks we allow ourselves to really enter into life, is something that some people seem to grasp quite naturally. For many of us, however, it can take a long time before we finally get there. Marianne Williamson in her book *A Return To Love* wrote: 'Our deepest fear is not that we are inadequate. Our deepest fear is that we are powerful beyond measure. It is our light, not our darkness that most frightens us.' Nelson Mandela famously used this quote to illustrate how we often fear our potential to be everything we can be. Learning to love our light, living with passion and commitment, is worth every knockback, every disappointment and every mistake; because we finally learn to value ourselves. Once we have achieved this, we then value everyone and everything around us.

The more we value life – all life – the more confident we feel. The more confident we feel about ourselves, the more confident we feel about other people. We enter a virtuous circle, where our compassion and confidence in ourselves is reflected in our compassion and confidence in others. In the decision matrix that is life, we have found the win–win formula.

Now I really wanted to experiment with my life, push the boundaries of what was comfortable and safe, and explore everything that came my way. Importantly, I would also accept help whenever possible, knowing that without a helping hand, life can be very difficult. I found that the more I helped others, the more I developed the capacity to be more accepting of the help that I also needed.

I ventured out of my life of ill health, tentatively taking up opportunities that I would previously have felt unworthy or incapable of rising to. Each time a possibility presented itself, instead of backing away from it in fear, I accepted it wholeheartedly. I learned to say 'Yes' instead of 'No', trusting that being me would be enough. Living with integrity and always trying to do my very best would see me through whatever lay ahead. What I discovered was that showing respect and loving compassion to those I came into contact with would generate opportunities and adventures that I had only dreamed of in the past.

I began to dare to be myself – as best I could – because I now liked and trusted myself enough to believe that this would be sufficient to get me started. I had finally developed a relationship with myself that would allow me to let go of the rigid confines of self-doubt.

And with every new challenge that I dared to accept, I discovered that confidence is not just something that happens after a success; it is something that sustains you through whatever challenges you face, no matter what the outcome. It is just as much, if not more so, the process as the content, the journey as the destination, that creates confidence and resilience.

Let's think about the myth of confidence for a moment and see how we can develop it as a skill to draw on when we need it most. We know that confidence is irresistible and inspirational; it is something that we all want; we love it in our celebrities, figureheads and leaders, and yet for ourselves it often feels elusive and transient. We have days when we feel more confident, yet others when we feel anything but. It is almost as if, once we have had a delicious taste of it, it appears determined to elude us, until seemingly randomly, it once more emerges, giving us a tantalising sense of how life would be if we experienced this marvellous state all the time. And yes, unfortunately, there are some of us who have never truly felt confident and wonder if we ever will.

Confidence is not something that just happens to us because life is treating us well. Even if life is treating us well – although this undoubtedly help foster confidence – there's no guarantee that we will feel self-assured. Sometimes when we are at our most successful, perversely we feel at our least confident, becoming anxiously aware of what we have to lose if we should fail. Why is creating and sustaining confidence so problematic? I think in part it is because it is a commitment that requires resolution and dedication: ultimately, it is a commitment to ourselves.

Committing to ourselves, however, is not easy. We find lots of reasons not to. Rather like taking exercise: we know we should, but we don't always want to. We say to ourselves, 'I'll go for my walk when I feel better, when I feel up to it ...' and then wonder why that time never comes, and end up feeling regretful. If we make ourselves go to the gym, however, we never regret it, knowing that we will feel better afterwards. As with exercise, the more we commit to ourselves, the more we respond to the reward of feeling better, so the more we want to continue. It is this commitment to our autonomy, to taking responsibility for ourselves, that is the key to creating confidence.

To build self-confidence, we can start to relate to ourselves with commitment and compassion in three key areas: trusting and accepting ourselves, having a positive, nurturing relationship with ourselves, and developing resilience. I would like to offer three different exercises for each of these areas of your life for you to explore.

### Trust and accept yourself

For most of us, the ideas we have about ourselves are formed by the experiences we have had and the messages we have received about ourselves from others. The problem with this is that, unless the majority of our experiences and messages have been positive, which is unlikely, we tend to remember the critical and negative experiences and messages far more.

Dr John Gottman[9] discovered in marital relationships that are healthy, for one negative event to be ameliorated, five positives have to occur – this is known as the Gottman ratio. If we speculate how this research might impact on having a healthy relationship with ourselves, it suggests that if we frequently internalise and believe the negative while dismissing the positive, just as a marriage is destroyed, we destroy ourselves, eroding our self-esteem and damaging our self-confidence. Only when we work to overcome our negative internal dialogue by attending to the many neglected positives we possess, will we develop resilience and self-assurance.

One approach is to stop waiting for external validation – a rare thing anyway, as most people are overly preoccupied with themselves and forget to validate others – and start loving and accepting yourself as you are now while imagining who you want to be in the future. In this way, you will get closer to the realisation that what *you* think about *yourself* is what really matters and is the first step to rediscovering your confidence.

### Trust and Accept Yourself Exercise

In this first exercise, write down in your journal all the things that you value about yourself now. To get you started, try answering some of these questions:

- People have often said that I am good at . . .
- My closest friends value me for my . . .

[9] J.M. Gottman & N. Silver, *The Seven Principles for Making Marriage Work: A Practical Guide* (Three Rivers Press, 2000)

- If I were to choose my top five favourite things about me, they would be . . .
- I might not be perfect but I know that I am special because . . .

Include any qualities, feelings, thoughts, activities or relationships that matter to you and that you care about, for these are integral to your self-worth too. If your mind wanders to the negative, remind yourself that this isn't helpful; this exercise is not about listing your faults, it is about defining your qualities, or what, in Positive Psychology, are known as signature strengths. If you find this exercise hard, imagine what your best friend would say about you in answer to these questions and again, notice what you value in yourself and what you care about most.

*Create a positive and confident relationship with yourself*
The next step in rediscovering your confidence is to begin to relate to yourself from a place of warm, positive, unconditional self-regard, something I hope the first exercise has inspired in you. If your internal dialogue is full of self-criticism, recrimination and regret, insidiously you are eroding your self-worth and destroying any chance you have of feeling good about yourself. So often we set ourselves unrelentingly, unrealistic perfectionist standards that create stress and anxiety. We also begin to think that other people perceive us in the way we perceive ourselves, with harsh and critical judgement, which further undermines our self-esteem. In changing how we relate to ourselves, removing the barriers to self-acceptance, we can begin to realise that in this moment we are just fine, we have done nothing wrong, and we are doing our best.

The more we allow ourselves to stay in the present moment, the less likely we are to be at the mercy of unhelpful ruminations about past experiences and the more able we are to connect to the possibility of relating to ourselves with positive acceptance. One of the ways that we help relate to ourselves from a loving and compassionate place is to imagine how we want to perceive ourselves and our lives. As Epictetus, the brilliant Greek philosopher said, 'First say to yourself what you would be; and then do what you have to do.'

## Create a Positive and Confident Relationship with Yourself Exercise

Continue working with your journal. Following on from listing all the things you value in yourself and all the things you care about in your life, answer the following questions:

- Being a positive and confident person would mean this ... to my self-image
- Being a positive and confident person would change my life in these ways ...
- Being a positive and confident person would mean I would perceive myself as ...
- Being a positive and confident person would mean others perceive me as ...
- Being a positive and confident person would allow me to ...

Again, if self-doubt, negativity or harsh self-criticism arises in your thinking, put these thoughts to one side as being unhelpful and return to the task. Focus is essential if we are to retrain our minds and create a more helpful relationship with ourselves.

### Develop resilience

Confidence, as I suggested earlier, is something that comes and goes. Sometimes it takes very little to give us a boost: a new haircut, a friendly compliment or talking to a good friend can remind us that we do invest in and take care of ourselves, that we are important and we do matter. But quite easily, this nascent confidence can be snatched away, seemingly arbitrarily. Something minor, for example, goes wrong with our day and we find ourselves in free-fall, doubting and feeling bad about ourselves. This is where the idea of committing to nurturing this aspect of ourselves is essential. As I mentioned earlier, just as we have to make ourselves go on our walk to feel the benefits, we have to commit to challenging self-destructive negativity and promoting positivity in ourselves.

The more we do this, the more we can influence the way our minds work. Remember that creating new neural pathways can take as little as three weeks. By consistently investing in ourselves and building our self-confidence through reflecting on what we value and care about in ourselves, we can create a self-confidence neural net which, if we feed it with nurturing thoughts, will strengthen and grow. As we create, feed and grow these positive neural nets, we begin to starve our negative cognitive pathways that thrive on self-criticism and doubt, until eventually these unhelpful neural nets will shrivel up and die off.

Resilience has been shown to be a quality that is protective when faced with adversity. American cognitive psychologist

Christine Padesky[10] has researched and developed a resilience model to help people overcome depression. This can be adapted to assist us when we find ourselves facing a problem that seems hard to overcome.

Life will not stop throwing things at us, so developing resilience is essential if we are to weather the inevitable vicissitudes of our daily experience. This is something all of us are liable to need during the difficult economic times we currently face. The exercises that follow will help you to discover your innate resilience and allow you to tap into it on a daily basis, to re-affirm your commitment to building confidence.

## Developing Your Resilience Exercises

The characteristics of resilience include being able to bounce back from adverse situations and having a 'can-do' attitude to life. Explore the following questions and give examples for each. In this way you will begin to see that your resilience is present; it simply needs to be acknowledged. If you find you are unable to answer any of these questions positively, do not despair. Imagine what it would take to produce a positive response and then identify the steps required to get you there. If, for example, you do not have a warm and nurturing social network, begin to invest in friendship by creating opportunities to meet new people and accepting any invitations that will broaden your friendship group.

[10] K.A. Mooney & C.A. Padesky, 'Applying client creativity to recurrent problems: Constructing possibilities and tolerating doubt', *Journal of Cognitive Psychotherapy: An International Quarterly*, 14:2 (2000), 149–161.

**EXERCISE 1** – *Identifying opportunities to develop resilience.*
In your journal, work through these questions in the spirit of loving, compassionate self-acceptance:

- Can I see problems as opportunities? Give examples . . .
- Can I cope when life gets tough? Give examples . . .
- Can I be flexible in different situations? Give examples . . .
- Do I make the most of what comes my way? Give examples . . .
- Do I have things in my life that give it meaning? Give examples . . .
- Do I have a warm and nurturing social support network? Give examples . . .

**EXERCISE 2** – *Identifying when you have activated your innate resilience.*
Now, identify a time in your life when you were faced with something challenging, then answer the following questions:

- In the past I faced —— and was able to overcome it by . . .
- Overcoming this challenge showed me that I had these qualities that I care about . . .
- I surprised myself when I . . .
- If faced with the same challenge I now know that I could . . .
- The most important thing I learned from this challenge was my ability to . . .

To give you an example, in answering these questions myself, I identified that in the past I have faced frightening and confusing episodes of ill health. Eventually, and with much reflection, I was able to overcome these experiences through a combination of resourcefulness, patience, resilience and empathy with others. It wasn't easy, and there were moments when I felt very afraid, distressed, overwhelmed and unhappy. But I can also see that these were all entirely appropriate feelings, given what I was going through.

Despite this, I feel fortunate to have had these experiences, because they taught me that I cared deeply about these attributes, discovering that, the more I invested in them, the more confident I felt. I surprised myself when I was able to deal with each successive problem with increasing compassion for myself and for those trying to help me, and this proved pivotal in my acceptance of what had happened and my ability to let go and not let these experiences define me negatively.

If faced with these challenges again, I would do what I have done before, hopeful that my resilience would support me through whatever occurred. The most important thing I have learned from these challenges is to show myself compassion, for without compassion, these experiences would have felt very cruel and overwhelming.

**EXERCISE 3** – *Identify confident, resilient role models.*
Finally, note down in your journal any role model from the past or present who exemplifies the qualities that you admire and would like for yourself. They could be people who have overcome seemingly overwhelming adversity, like Helen Keller, or who actualised themselves in an extraordinarily beautiful way, like Audrey Hepburn, or inspired a nation, like Mandela or Ghandi. They could be your mother, father or sibling; they could be your best friend. Capture what it is about those people that inspires you and then incorporate into your own way of being those qualities that you most

desire for yourself. For myself, my aunt Andrea was a guiding light during my illnesses. She had died tragically young from breast cancer and all through her terrible illness, she was beautiful, brave and gentle. Much loved and missed by all her family, to us she was an icon of resilience and fortitude in the face of terrible suffering.

When you feel your confidence slipping, remind yourself of your role model and ask yourself what they would do if they were feeling the way you are. In this way, you can internalise a mentor – a protective role model – who can help inspire you to tap into your resilience and step into a more positive attitude, to see you through the challenges you face.

One area in which we often let our sense of not feeling confident get the better of us is in social situations. We love people, we enjoy being around them, we desire and need their company, yet even the most extrovert of us can feel uncertain in new social situations. This anxiety is normal, often generated because we fear that we may be judged. Being found wanting is a universal source of apprehension which many of us carry simply because we judge ourselves too harshly. Being our own worst critics, we undermine our self-esteem, projecting into our social environment the belief that if we feel negatively about ourselves then others will too and we will be rejected. In many cases, this becomes a self-fulfilling prophecy which further justifies our fears.

To alleviate this social anxiety, one of the most helpful steps we can take is identify what it is that we most value. By focusing on what gives our lives meaning we can develop a core sense of self that reduces our need for external validation, because we have created a strong sense of what we value in ourselves. For example, my core values are to be caring, understanding, compassionate and loving. These are the values that I aspire to bring to all my social interactions, even when I am having a difficult day. Knowing that this is how I want to be, I feel less at the mercy of negatively paranoid thinking. If I am trying to be these things then I know I am doing my best. Trusting this, I am not prey to censuring myself and can instead turn my attention to the needs of those who surround me. By thinking about them, I can be more of who I really want to be, which in turn helps me feel relaxed and self-assured.

Mirroring positive feelings about ourselves in all our communications is a powerful quality that instantly puts others at their ease. Even the shyest person can create for themselves a social identity that allows their core values to shine. We don't have to be the chattiest, most entertaining person in the room: having a quiet, gentle presence can often be more attractive because the quality of the energy we are reflecting is so welcoming and open, drawing people closer.

Feeling good about our unique qualities and attributes can make us wonderful companions, because it frees us to listen and be attentive to others. Nothing is more engaging than showing genuine interest in another person. It is always appreciated. We have one mouth and two ears: if we listen for twice as long as we talk, not only will we learn much about how other people are feeling, but we also give them our time. Time is one of the most precious commodities we have and sharing our time generously by giving others our full attention is one of the most caring things we can do. If you find talking at parties difficult, remember that everyone needs someone who will listen and you will always be valued highly for having this often neglected skill.

The more in tune you are with your own internal set of beliefs, the less you will be distressed by perceived slights and careless words. It is always helpful to remember that everyone else also has their own pet preoccupations and we should not take things so personally. Things we think may be about us – their distraction, disinterest, distance or irritability – are usually about something that is happening to them.

You could also alleviate any self-conscious anxieties by reminding yourself that because everyone is self-absorbed to an extent, they will rarely notice any fluffs you might have made. Even if they did, they won't mind: their thoughts will very quickly be returning to themselves. By showing an empathic awareness that all of us are in this situation together, we can begin to release the fear of being judged and enjoy being in company. These are simply people, who, like all of us, want to get along and have an enjoyable time.

Before you leave for a social engagement, prime yourself with some gentle words of encouragement for yourself and the people you are going to meet. Remind yourself that bringing along harsh self-criticisms about who you are or what you look like will not set you up for a good time. Put aside your doubts and bring with you the values and qualities you care about instead. Being warm, open, responsive and kind will always attract others to you, before you have said anything at all. Practising a half-smile before we enter the room will create a positive mindset, wherever we go and whoever we talk to.

Confidence, like happiness, is a state of mind that is rarely contingent on external events. The most confident person I have ever met was a young Indian boy who burst into my train carriage in Mumbai and performed a delightful, creative and amusing song and dance routine, using only two flat stones that he clapped together castanet style. Despite clearly having nothing, probably not even parents, he radiated energy, humour, charm and above all self-confidence. He had learnt to be confident because he had no choice. Confidence fed him, it was a necessary part of his life that helped him survive. Already, aged seven or eight, he had learned this vital lesson through hardship: confidence was his friend. He had nothing to lose by being confident regardless of the potential outcome, but he had everything to lose if he did not try. Giving him rupees to buy food, I thought to myself, *If he can do it, then surely so can I.* And so can we all.

## Week Seven

**Cognitive**

Continue to capture pleasant events in your journal. By now you should be more aware of the triggers for unpleasant events and have a more compassionate relationship with them. If any new ones arise, process them in your journal just as you have done before, adding to your self-knowledge as you do so. You should also continue to observe your thoughts as just thoughts and not facts.

Every day this week, do one of the exercises suggested in this chapter. You can start with the 'Trust and accept yourself' exercise and then move on to 'Create a positive and confident relationship with yourself'. Then attempt the three resilience exercises. Keep a record in your journal and reflect on your responses. Acknowledge any moments of confidence and resilience that arise during the week and note them down in your journal. The more you recognise these attributes in yourself, the more you will be able to call on them when you need them most.

**Behavioural**

Choose an activity this week that you have never attempted before and may even be a little afraid of. It could be a physical activity such as doing a ropes course, scaling a climbing wall, going to a yoga class or having a swimming lesson. Or it could be a mental challenge, such as filling in a cryptic crossword or Sudoku puzzle. The idea is to stick at your task until you begin to feel more confident with it. Always remember that, when in doubt, give yourself time to reflect rather than react. Be firm but gentle with yourself. You are not in competition with yourself; you are learning to develop your sense of confidence and your ability to be resilient.

Additionally, remember to continue with your mindfulness practice, choosing one thing you do each day to engage in with complete awareness. Continue to use the breathing space at the set points during the day and for coping when feeling tired, overwhelmed or stressed. Continue to use your bodyscan meditation. The more you practise, the better you will feel.

I hope that you are still walking and eating for your well-being. This should now be so well established that you will notice if you forget and your body will miss the nurturing attention you have been giving yourself.

### Emotional

Make a note in your journal recording anything you noticed in yourself when undergoing the challenging experience. Note any moments of anxiety, self-doubt or criticism and reflect on what you did in those moments. Also write down any sensations of confidence and resilience you experienced and how they felt to you emotionally.

Find a picture of your role model and stick it in your journal. Write about how they make you feel, what they inspire in you and what qualities in them you would like to emulate. Refer back to your role model whenever you are despondent or feel like quitting.

## Cognitive Reframe: Control Issues

Many of us take a quiet pride in our control issues, not only because they mean we are self-aware, but also because they mirror our craving for perfection. Our need for control is also activated by contemporary reality, in that so much of our experience feels chaotic due to overpowering technological intrusion. The desire actively to pursue control makes sense to us because otherwise we are in danger of feeling overwhelmed. It provides a means of psychologically containing that which feels uncontainable while masking our insecurities.

The demands made by working long hours, combined with information saturation, leave us obsessively trying to control what little we can influence directly ourselves, which sadly often means our relationships. Additionally, the immediacy of technology confronts us with global catastrophes, so we feel scarily unsafe, despite statistically never having been safer. Control therefore becomes a touchstone – I control therefore I am in control – but the more we try to control, the more out of control we feel, because we are asking the impossible. Women are particularly vulnerable, because we often combine work with family duties, trying to do both perfectly, flooding us with responsibilities. The fear of losing control when overburdened twists rapidly into being over-controlling to compensate.

The key to skilfully managing our control issues is to accept that we have them and then learn to let go of them when they stop being helpful to us. When faced with controlling relationships, we can soften our position and accept that our friends also have issues of control that, if we are honest, we recognise in ourselves. We then no longer have to struggle for ownership of control because, in reality, it is a shared experience. We have to accept that the perfect, beautifully controlled life some of us desire is unrealistic, and in letting go, we move closer to actually enjoying the beautifully uncontrolled life we do have.

# 8
## Positive Psychology

I mentioned earlier the subject of Positive Psychology, and you might well have already heard of it. I would like to explore it a little further, because it holds some helpful and constructive approaches to life that are relevant when forming a resilient relationship with ourselves.

When Professor Martin Seligman, an eminent psychologist, turned his attention to what it is that makes us happy and fulfilled, he termed this new scientific discipline Positive Psychology. For research purposes, he systematically defined happiness as 'subjective wellbeing' and developed a formula to describe the components that create subjective wellbeing: the degree of happiness we can experience (H), is determined by our biological predisposition to be happy, called the 'set point' (S), combined with the conditions of our lives (C), and the voluntary activities we choose to be involved in (V). His formula for happiness, therefore, is $H = S + C + V$.

If our biological set point is at a level where it takes very little to make us happy, we are indeed fortunate. Some of us, however, might not be so genetically blessed, which might make feeling happy quite a challenge, even if we enjoy many favourable conditions combined with freedom of choice.

Conditions are comprised of the things we have, such as our work, finances, housing and holidays; yet they also consist of the things we cannot change about ourselves, such as our sex, race and age, whether we are in a relationship, recently bereaved, are physically well or have illnesses or disabilities that compromise our health.

New research suggests that we can actively take steps to alter the set point at which we started. In other words, even if we are biologically programmed to require much to make us feel happy, we can retrain our minds to lower the bar to a level that is more manageable. We can learn to become satisfied with less to feel good about ourselves.

The conditions of our life – as we have explored before, and, as all of us will have experienced – will never be perfect. We can improve our sense of wellbeing, however, by accepting the realities of our life 'conditions'. That does not mean we cannot strive to improve our lot, but we do not have to be angry, disappointed or upset with ourselves if we do not have everything we think we should have. Accepting who and what we are right now will release energy that might otherwise be bound up in regret, recrimination or pernicious admonition to do better; liberating us to truly enjoy what we already have and work towards what we dream of.

Additionally, by accepting that our biological set point for happiness can sometimes feel a bit of a struggle, we can understand and forgive ourselves if we don't feel happy all the time. It's therapeutic to realise that it's normal to feel neutral, low or sad in the presence of losses or stressors; it's all part of our rich emotional experience and these feelings can and will pass, as all feelings eventually do.

The things we *choose* to do create a healthy balance with

the things we *have* to do. It seems obvious, yet how many of us actually manifest this principle in our lives? Taking time for ourselves to exercise, socialise, meditate, relax, engage in our community, learn something new, go travelling – anything, in fact, that we have chosen for ourselves because it makes us feel good – will optimise our sense of wellbeing and add to our happiness quotient. This can feel selfish, but in fact the opposite is true.

Research[11] shows that the more we give of ourselves to others the happier we feel, but to be altruistic we need internal resources of goodwill, which we create and maintain by choosing wisely for ourselves. The sense of wellbeing our choices create in us enables us to give more to others. Choosing activities to sustain wellbeing also requires an investment. This means that unlike the conditions of our lives that we adapt to very quickly and then take for granted, our voluntary activities retain an 'alive' quality, which when internalised can make a tangibly positive difference to the way we feel about ourselves.

There are some conditions, such as age and disability, that we cannot change. In accepting the reality of these fixed conditions, we can free up energy to make changes where

[11] See for example (with thanks to www.pursuit-of-happiness.org):

Stephen G. Post, 'Altruism and Happiness: It's Good to Be Good', *International Journal of Behavioral Medicine*, 12:2 (2005), 66–77

K.I. Hunter & M.W. Linn, *International Journal of Aging and Human Development*, 12 (1980–1981), 205–213

M.A. Musick & J. Wilson, 'Volunteering and depression: The role of psychological and social resources in different age groups', *Social Science & Medicine*, 56 (2003), 259–269

R.F. Krueger, B.M. Hicks & M. McGue, 'Altruism and antisocial behavior: Independent tendencies, unique personality correlates, distinct etiologies', *Psychological Science*, 12 (2001), 397–402.

we can. Research has shown that there are a number of external conditions that make a difference to our levels of happiness. One of these is commuting. Commuting erodes our happiness quotient because it markedly contributes to stress levels. People who commute long distances arrive at work with higher levels of stress hormones than people who live close to work. Reduce your commute as much as possible, even if it means living in smaller accommodation. We don't really need a large amount of physical living space, but we do need plenty of 'internal space' to have time for the voluntary activities that improve our wellbeing. Being stuck in traffic or on an overcrowded train twice a day, five days a week, frays our sense of wellbeing, diminishing opportunities to cultivate happiness.

Jonathon Haidt in his excellent book, *The Happiness Hypothesis*,[12] notes that research also shows that we can never completely adapt to new or chronic noise pollution. Loud noises trigger one of our earliest fear responses (the other is the fear of falling) and we never fully relax if we are surrounded by intermittent or persistently intrusive noise. Noisy neighbours are one of the most emotive causes of domestic upset in our communities for very good reason: many of us simply cannot adapt to them.

Realising that there are really very few fixed variables that have a lasting impact on our sense of wellbeing gives us the knowledge that, if we choose to invest wisely in our lives, we can make considerable changes towards lasting happiness. Seligman, in his groundbreaking book *Authentic Happiness*,[13]

[12] J. Haidt, *The Happiness Hypothesis* (Arrow Books, 2006)
[13] M. Seligman, *Authentic Happiness* (Nicholas Brealey Publishing, 2003)

identifies what he calls signature strengths, mentioned earlier, that we can all cultivate to improve our sense of wellbeing. Underpinning these strengths are six human characteristics he calls 'virtues': wisdom, courage, humanity, justice, temperance and transcendence. Seligman clusters attributes around each of these virtues to help identify what our signature strengths are. Attributes such as curiosity in the world that surrounds us, open-mindedness, ingenuity, originality of thinking, social, personal and emotional intelligence and a sense of perspective are all clustered under the virtues of 'Wisdom and Knowledge'.

The virtue of 'Humanity' for example, contains the attributes of kindness and generosity, the ability to love and be loved, and I would also include here a sense of compassion. 'Transcendence' is a virtue that could also be called spirituality, but that term is so overused as to be almost meaningless now. Transcendence captures the qualities of being human that make us very special: our appreciation of beauty and excellence and our sense of gratitude, which has been shown to have a huge impact on our emotional health. Hope and optimism also fall under this virtue, as do forgiveness and mercy, playfulness, humour, passion and enthusiasm. This is one of my favourites of all the virtues and one in which I believe we can make the most difference to our personal sense of wellbeing after loving and being loved.

The most important of all the external conditions that can improve our happiness quotient is that of having relationships.[14] Fulfilling, reciprocal, loving and gentle

[14] See research examples at http://pursuit-of-happiness.org/sciencehappiness.aspx

relationships can do more to uplift our experience of happiness than all the other conditions put together. Often our deepest sources of unhappiness are found in poor relationships with others. A colleague at work who bullies, undermines or dismisses our feelings, creates untold wretchedness. A conflictual relationship with a lover leaves us feeling betrayed and abandoned. A relationship with our parents or children, not based on compassionate unconditional positive regard, creates misunderstanding and misery.

We never fully adapt to hostile relationships. They invidiously contaminate our wellbeing even if we are not in physical contact with the source of our distress, as they squat inside our minds as unresolved, repetitious ruminations. When faced with relationships such as these, the most constructive and positive thing we can do is to either mend the relationship or move on, letting go our upset in the process.

As with all our relationships, we need to invest if we are to flourish. Once again, the one key relationship that we must invest in, if all our other relationships are to succeed, is the one we have with ourselves. This message is worth repeating over and over, as it is the one relationship we most often neglect.

Imagine that your emotional wellbeing, or if you prefer, your sense of happiness, is like a very special bank. Into this bank we deposit experiences that have given us pleasure, have made us feel good, and that have made us feel loved and loving. We can also include as beneficial deposits: acknowledging our successes, not diminishing or denying our achievements, taking satisfaction in a job well done or effort wisely expended, and bringing commitment and passion to all that we love.

As we have discussed before, we have a tendency to remember negative events and dismiss positive events, not acknowledging them or recalling them when times are hard. This possibly came about as an evolutionary adaptation to assist our survival in hostile environments, but it can hinder our sense of wellbeing by leaving us with an emotional deficit and a skewed perspective of how our lives really are. When we savour our positive experiences and deposit them in our bank of wellbeing, we create reserves that we can draw on when we are stressed, overwhelmed, bereaved, misunderstood or unlucky in love. It's important that we invest wisely, because if we fail to notice the good things in our lives and account for them, carefully placing them in the strongroom that is our heart, then when we need to make a withdrawal, there will be nothing there.

It might also be the case that we do try to invest, we do try to savour and cultivate a wealth of resources, but we are constantly paying out to other relationships that do not sustain us in return. Relationships that make consistent withdrawals, running up debt – like an overdraft without collateral on our wellbeing account – are exhausting and depleting. At some point we need to address this and think about whether these are relationships that are good for us to be in.

The more we have invested in ourselves – the more we have acknowledged, appreciated, valued and felt compassion for ourselves – the healthier our balance will be. We are then in a very good position to be altruistic; allowing others to make withdrawals for themselves, which in turn makes us feel good and adds to our own store, accruing interest. But we must be aware that when we are going through difficult times we will have to withdraw reserves for ourselves and not spread our outgoings too thinly. We need to ensure that we have a savings account; one in which the sum total of our wellbeing is protected by continuing to take care of ourselves and be wise with our expenditure. It is at these times that we can turn to our friends, knowing that, because we have also invested in them, they will have reserves of wellbeing to help us out. In time, when we have recovered, our books will once more be balanced and we can resume our usual commerce of trading wellbeing with those we love and care about.

In many ways, those we love and care about should include everyone we come into contact with. Our GP, dentist, dry cleaner, corner-shop owner, postie, bus driver, elderly neighbour, friend's children, street sweeper, even our parking-enforcement officer deserves to have a wellbeing bank deposit whenever we connect with them. What we receive in return might well be variable, depending on their own rates of wellbeing 'interest', but we do not need to take this personally. They might be having a bad day or their own emotional bank account might be in the red, and it is then that our compassion can override our instinct to judge and blame. Instead, we can stay with our intention: that we pay in gladly, spending without expectation.

By paying in freely, every now and then we get a most rewarding dividend – a surprise bonus. That bonus can be a friendly smile, a shared glimmer of understanding or a cheerful exchange about the weather. Those who dismiss chats about the weather among strangers as banal or boring are missing a fundamental point: they are simply a safe way of connecting with people by showing that we are friendly, open and we care. They are important conversations in their own way because the intention, the underlying sentiment behind them, is of far greater magnitude than the content.

These simple moments of human connection help make sense of everything in our seemingly senseless world. The more we invest positively in others, the better we all feel, and the more others invest positively in us, the better we all feel. This perfect symmetry, surely, is beautiful and wise.

Another aspect where we can draw on Positive Psychology is to create more of a sense of control in our lives. Sometimes life does feel horribly out of control. The sense that you are not in command of your future creates anxiety and, if left unchecked, can lead to low mood. There are six fundamental psychological requirements that must be met if we are to feel stable and content: physical and emotional security, economic wellbeing, a sense of belonging and recognition and, of course, control over our lives. Right now, facing an uncertain economic future, many of us will be feeling that at least three of our basic needs are being compromised. Our sense of security is closely tied to our economic wellbeing, and if these are threatened we start to feel more controlled and less in control. We may turn to comfort eating or spending in an effort to alleviate our anxiety – only to find life becoming increasingly unmanageable.

Although it can be tempting to ignore these fundamental needs, we cannot deny them because avoidance just adds to our sense of insecurity. For those of us who are feeling pressured because our carefully cultivated sense of independence, developed through hard work and commitment, is under threat, there are some tools we can use to regain equilibrium and focus on what matters and what truly helps. It is always worth remembering that we respond to the world not as it really is but the way we perceive it to be. Energy spent chasing worries can be seen as a natural, but self-defeating, distraction from finding more constructive solutions.

To overcome the feeling that everything is spiralling chaotically beyond our grasp, try reflecting for a moment on what is possible rather than automatically assuming the worst. Instead of focusing on what appears to be going wrong, focus on what is going right. As mentioned earlier, we can do this by identifying our strengths, which can all too often get forgotten, particularly if we are judging ourselves harshly because we fear we are not coping. Investing in our strengths will help us value ourselves and give us a sense of direction, which is crucial if we are going to feel more in control of our destiny.

Part of feeling uncontained is the sensation that we do not have enough time. Jon Kabat-Zinn in *Coming to our Senses*,[15] suggests that there are two mechanisms that we often resort to when attempting to alleviate the fear of time dissipating. We try to fill up our lives with as many novel experiences as possible, ultimately adding to our sense of feeling over-faced and overwhelmed. This strategy is so marvellously distracting that we momentarily forget our worries, only to find we have expended our resources by spreading ourselves too thin, with nothing left for the challenges we face.

Alternatively, we can slow down the impression of frenziedly escaping time by making more of the simple moments that are nurturing and fulfilling, such as turning off our TV, email and phone so as to be really present with our loved

[15] J. Kabat-Zinn, *Coming to Our Senses* (Piatkus, 2005)

ones, or as pioneering British psychiatrist, Professor Anne Farmer – tapping into similar ideas contained in the Slow Food[16] movement – once said to me, 'Make jam, it helps regain perspective!'

As the list of demands inexorably lengthens, we tend to prioritise everything but ourselves. Neglecting our own needs, however, diminishes our sense of self and can leave us feeling abandoned and forgotten. Making time for ourselves reinforces the idea that we are in control of our lives, because we are reminding ourselves that we matter, we count and are worth taking care of. Attending to our personal pleasures – our gym session, ballet class, choir practice or walk in the park – ensures that we stay in touch with what is healthy and balancing, particularly when life feels challenging. It is these simple, creative but life-affirming moments that reconnect us to our awareness of belonging, of 'being in it together', which helps us regain our sense of self.

Slowing down our lives by making time for ourselves creates a more balanced perspective. We begin to see that, although there may be tough times ahead, the elements in our lives we care about, the aspects that really matter, can and will remain stable: our love for our friends, family and children, our sense of purpose and the recreations we pursue that also give our lives meaning, such as music, art and literature, or simply baking a delicious cake.

This is because, whatever the external conditions of our lives – be it increased financial burdens, unwanted weight gain, unexpected redundancies – a core sense of autonomy will carry us bravely through to face the next day and the

[16] http://www.slowfood.com/

day after that. When a problem arises, we can take a step back, pause, breathe and create space around the issue so that we can reframe it as a challenge rather than a catastrophe.

Instead of instantly reacting, which sometimes results in hasty or irrational decisions because we feel pressured, we can adopt a third position and bear witness to our predicament. We can ask ourselves to reflect on what is occurring and give ourselves permission to take time to think and work towards a solution, using small, manageable goals to guide us.

This might feel risky at first, because we have an urge to fix things immediately. The reality, fortunately, is that there is little in life that is polarised in a black-versus-white, life-or-death context. Taking time to reflect opens up the possibility of a creative, lateral response, again supporting the idea that we have more control than we realise in the choices we make.

For example, you might not be able to afford to take your family abroad next summer, but you could take your children on a working farm holiday instead. Their pleasure will be just as great and you can fulfil your personal ambition to be more environmentally aware and teach your children about the countryside. An internal sense of control, sustained by the belief that we are doing our best, that we can and will cope by holding on to, or finding, those vital kernels of inspiration and hope, whatever our experience holds, can help us manage the many challenges ahead.

None of us want to feel totally out of control. When we do, the slightest obstacle can appear overwhelming. But by confronting rather than avoiding the issues, we can all make a stake in an optimistic future, taking a reflective rather than a reactive look at what is happening, and adapt accordingly by developing flexible, positive and meaningful responses. We may even surprise ourselves, discovering that by cultivating a deep sense of ownership of our lives we can face even the toughest adversity with humour, grace and style.

One exercise derived from Positive Psychology is to show gratitude on a daily basis by writing down, every evening, three or more good things that happened to you during the day. These things can be very straightforward: they do not have to be fancy, amazing or materially based events. They could be as simple as enjoying that first perfect cup of coffee or tea in the morning, listening to birdsong or watching a sunset. They could be a sweet smile from your child, a kiss from your partner, or a word of encouragement from your colleague at work. They could be a funny joke, an interesting article, or a telephone call from someone you have been thinking about. (This exercise differs from capturing pleasant and unpleasant events, the purpose of which is to distinguish the alternate thoughts, feelings and physical sensations, rather than a simple act of gratitude.)

By beginning to distinguish the good things that happen to us throughout the course of a day, noting them down and savouring them, we start to build up that reservoir of good feeling that sustains us. It might seem a simple task; for some, it will appear too simple, raising the question, 'How could that possibly help?' But many people have found it to be incredibly useful in regaining perspective, thinking about their lives differently and lifting their mood. By listing the things that have happened that have made us feel good, we start to notice that no one day is all bad, that even when we are stressed, rushed, tired or ill, there are moments of reprieve that punctuate our day; we just need to be open to noticing them.

## Week Eight

**Cognitive**
In your journal every evening write down three good things that happened during the day that you can be grateful for. You may want to continue to record your pleasant and unpleasant events, but remember these are about capturing the physical as well as mental sensations that arose in you. The three moments of gratitude are just that, events that made you feel grateful, warm inside and happy.

You should now be able to thought record in your head routinely. There will always be sticky areas in your thinking, however, and it helps to remember that this is normal. When it happens, get out your thought record and process it, just as you would any other problem. You will become increasingly aware there are some thought processes that cannot be resolved with a thought record. Again, this is normal. A thought record cannot bring back a lost love, a missed opportunity or fix an unhappy childhood. What it can do, however, is change the way in which you relate to these realities, freeing you up to experience yourself now, in this present moment. Any issues that cannot be resolved with a thought record require you to acknowledge, accept and let go.

**Behavioural**
Write a simple letter of gratitude to someone who deserves it. It could be your teacher, your friend, your boss at work, the dinner lady or the friendly couple across the street who

look after your spare keys. Show them you appreciate them, without expecting anything back. The more grateful we are for what we have, the happier we are. A skilful definition of happiness is wanting what we have and not wanting what we don't have.

Do one positive thing for yourself every day this week. Find ways of rewarding yourself that are nurturing and life-enhancing. Gaze out over your favourite view, listen to a beautiful piece of music, lay a beautiful table, tidy your desk. The list of positive things we can do for ourselves (and for others) is endless. Let your imagination break free. Do this practice every day and you may find yourself taking a creative course, climbing a mountain or changing your career!

Continue to walk for half an hour daily, swim or practise yoga and eat your wellbeing foods. Keep up your mindfulness practice and use the breathing space three times a day and for coping. If you have found the bodyscan meditation helpful, continue to practise, knowing that you are giving yourself special time every day to centre yourself and keep your reserves of wellbeing in tip-top condition.

**Emotional**

Find more creative ways to tell the people in your life that you love them. Words are powerful, actions even more so. Draw a picture, or if you are no artist, find a picture that expresses how you feel. Make a CD of their favourite music. Take them on a walk that means something to both of you. Talk about the experience as you do so, why you are there, why it matters. Sharing ourselves in this way brings intimacy and untold joy. Remember to write it up in your journal, memories such as these are worth saving, creating that reservoir of wellbeing that will feed us when we face more challenging times.

Continue to tell the people in your life that you love them. Life is too short not to hear these precious words and too often they are held back. Why? Because we are afraid to risk saying them for fear of making ourselves look foolish, weak, needy or whatever the story is. Yet love is free, it costs us nothing and the more we give, the more we receive. Give without expectation.

At this point in the programme, your relationship with yourself should feel softer, lighter, gentler, and increasingly vital. Your judging mind will now be under your control, not vice versa, and your ability to think fluidly and creatively about your life will continue to develop the deeper you take your practice using the skills and tools you have discovered over the eight weeks of workshops. You are nearing the end of this process. Acknowledge how far you have come with a reward that is just for you. Choose one of the activities that you have found really helpful over the last eight weeks, clear an hour in your schedule and devote that hour to yourself without interruption.

Begin to choose which skills, tools and exercises have resonated most clearly for you throughout this eight-week journey and that you have found to be the most beneficial. Commit to keeping these helpful practices in your life. Revisit them frequently to preserve your sense of wellbeing and to remind yourself that the more you invest in yourself, the more resources you will have to invest in your life and the lives of others.

## Cognitive Reframe: Positive Interactions

Interact with one new person every day this week, whether it be a friendly 'Hello', a 'Can I help you?' or simply a big, beaming smile. Note how you feel, before, during and after the interaction. If you value how you feel as a result, continue to incorporate this friendly, open style of communicating every day. You might even find you make some new friends along the way.

An increased awareness and acknowledgement of gratitude has been shown to increase our sense of wellbeing and have a direct impact on the way in which we view ourselves and our lives. This simple exercise, if practised regularly, becomes a skill, teaching us to see our world with optimism and hope. We need these daily reminders that everything changes; each day yields up new moments of joy that, if dismissed, cannot be added to our reservoir of wellbeing, but if embraced, can change the way we feel about everything in a moment.

## Cognitive Reframe: Work

It is a common misconception that giving up work will make us feel better if we are feeling stressed or low. Yet those without work or meaningful endeavours are usually far more unhappy and unhealthy than those with. If there is nothing intrinsically wrong with the work you are doing, then it is your relationship to work that requires reflection.

One of Freud's least controversial attributed claims was that love and work are all that matter in life. Being passionate about what we do makes work a pleasure, becoming an expression of the way we want to live our lives. Think about what it is you bring to work – not your lunch, but your attitude! Ask yourself what your expectations are: of yourself, your work and your future. Do you experience work as a place where you learn, develop skills and complete tasks with satisfaction? If not, find yourself a mentor, someone who you trust and admire, someone who demonstrably loves what they do, and ask them to teach you how to love what you do, too.

It is all too easy to erode the important meaning that work gives us by endlessly complaining that we have to do it. For most of us, we *do* have to do it, so we might as well bring a little grace, dignity and good humour to it. Commit yourself to bringing to work all the qualities that you want to receive from it, such as creativity, goal achievement or caring for others. The more you embody these qualities, the more they will be reflected back to you. If you want trust, be trusting. If you want promotion, promote yourself and back it up with industry. If you long for innovation, be the first to be innovative; don't be afraid to take some risks. Be curious and spontaneous, and connect with your colleagues; witness how this can totally transform your day. As with all areas of life, the more we invest into the situation, the more we receive; a simple but true equation.

# 9

## Dare to Be You

There are two metaphors that help me stay in a world that is balanced, rich in potential and full of hope. These metaphors are of a garden and a bridge. As a child, one of my favourite books was *The Secret Garden* by Frances Hodgson Burnett. The eponymous garden has been neglected for a long time and a young girl, Mary, brings it back to life. In doing so, she transforms herself, overcoming her own misfortunes, becoming resilient through her new-found happiness because she has created something alive and beautiful through her powers of nurturance. Eventually, she develops the resources to help an unhappy boy, Colin, who is also in much need of nurturing and loving. The story is essentially about the transformative power of love. With love, life blossoms. Instead of seeking love outside ourselves, thinking that this will transform us, it is the love we show ourselves that is transformational.

I like to think about my internal world as being such a garden. There is a patch that I have dug around in for far too long, creating an empty hole: no light can reach into it and the birds do not sing here. Nothing grows, however hard I try. Over and over, I have prodded and poked at the heavy cloying soil, despairing at the strangling roots and weeds, hoeing excessively at the seedlings I have tried to plant there until they are battered and bruised, unable to flourish. Despite its unforgiving nature, it's hard to resist returning to this dead piece of ground. I keep trying to improve and fix it. If I could just work harder, do more and not give up, then somehow I will make it better. So much of my energy becomes invested here – even though there is not the slightest evidence that there is any point in continuing to work on it – that there is nothing left for the rest of the garden, which is longing for my attention.

Running wild, the rest of my garden is certainly overgrown and neglected, yet it is full of life, with the potential to be beautiful, sunny and rich in possibilities, with endless opportunities for growth and renewal. In remembering this, I then also remember that I am more than this sorry patch of ground that transfixes me, yet yields me nothing but the dead hand of the past. I am all that is possible, made manifest in the rest of my spacious garden, if only I would look around and see. But I don't know how to move over to the rest of my garden.

To transform ourselves, we need to begin to tell a different story about our lives. We know when we are telling an old story because it bores us: we feel tired; our voice lacks energy, becoming monotonous and whiney. We go on and on, hoping that by telling the story again, somehow it will all make sense to us, somehow we will get over it, somehow it will be fixed. But the story, which yes, might once have been full of emotions, still raw from whatever wound it has left us with, now leaves us cold from over-telling. It leaves our listeners cold as well, for however sympathetic they might be, they can sense that we have told this story many times before and there isn't going to be a happy ending. They feel drained by it, as it drains us. There is no solution, it cannot be fixed, it just is what it is: a story of our past, an old story, a story that is going nowhere.

To avoid our real feelings, we have often shrouded our story in a blanket of pointless guilt. Its only function is to obscure us from our sorrow for all the losses we have endured, perhaps the loss of an idealised family, or relationship, or a global sense of the loss of an idealised life. Most importantly, as it is all too easy to keep finding others to blame, our guilt is often about the loss of an idealised version of ourselves who wouldn't have made the mistakes we have made, who was somehow perfect.

Our guilt drips off us, oozing into our conversation, like an old and unlovely blanket that we are loath to burden our shoulders with but somehow cannot quite shake off. It smothers our other feelings, until we imagine we no longer have them. We become our guilt, and then feel depressed. Depressed, we feel even guiltier, and so these two miseries feed off each other. All too quickly we have lost hope; we believe we are the story we tell about ourselves and nothing else. We believe the myth that we are our thoughts and our thoughts are us.

Insidiously, we become our story. Eventually, we no longer even have to tell it; people can see it before we even open our mouths and begin to speak. We wear it in the furrows of our brow, the downturned edges of our mouth, the lifeless looks and anxious glances. Gradually we feel we cannot gaze upon anyone, and we look down, avoiding contact. We become isolated and locked in. How we hate our story – and soon we discover that we hate ourselves even more.

But if we were to divest ourselves of the past, we could become flooded with relief as we rid ourselves of guilt's clammy grip. For a moment, we might feel exposed, naked and vulnerable without our old story to hide behind. But now we have a chance to see ourselves more clearly. No longer hidden from ourselves, we can take a look at what our past has prevented us from mourning and begin the process of transformation.

Acknowledging our losses, we can be gentle with our real feelings, accept them and show ourselves some much-needed compassion. Whatever we did then, we did it because we thought it was the right thing to do, or we thought we had no option, or we did it knowing it was wrong for us, but went ahead and did it anyway. Whatever the reason, we need to forgive ourselves now, accept that what's done is done and let it go. Instead of falling into despair, fear or regret, we can look ahead and build ourselves a bridge to help us cross over. We don't need to keep falling into the dark spaces of our minds. But if we do – and we will, because we are human and it is hard to make changes – we can remind ourselves that we are choosing to fall and we can stop it now, if we only do something different.

That difference can be as simple as valuing one thing in ourselves or our lives, and focusing our attention on that. We might identify that we value our creativity, or our sense of humour, or our warmth, or even better, all three. Instantly, we have the beginnings of a bridge – each virtue, attribute or strength representing a plank – a bridge that will get us across to the other side, without having to fall over and over. The planks of our bridge lead us to the other part of our garden that has been neglected for too long. It moves us away from the dead ground, carries us high over the dark or angry places, past the prickly events that make us sore, the stinging words that make us smart, the toxic moments that make us ill. With every plank we lay down, we take a step forward, into a new story.

However, often our anxiety about the future can make us stay down in this dark space, paralysed, unable to act because we *do not know*. Our assumptions about the future become increasingly catastrophic and terrifying, particularly if viewed through a lens of self-loathing. So we might stay in this twilight world for years, unable to take the risk and emerge to face our unknown future.

Yet with our bridge, we see where we are going (the final exercise in this chapter gives advice on how to construct your own bridge). We build it carefully, making sure that we do not drag the dead weight of the past on to it for fear of overloading it with assumptions and expectations. The past can stay down in the hole, where it belongs, along with meaningless guilt. As our bridge grows, we travel further and further away from our old story. Feeling more confident, our self-esteem recovers – for we are doing this for ourselves – we are creating this and it comes from a good place, from a wish to transform and live the life we really want.

We dare ourselves to venture along it, even if sometimes we have to cling to the handrail as a hailstorm of doubts beset us, or the high wind of uncertainty prevails. Eventually, we realise that our bridge is made up of many different aspects of ourselves that we have learned to value. The bridge is suspended from foundations based in love, trust, compassion and hope for ourselves. In living our own truth, these foundations become unshakeable, weathering the worst of storms; our bridge now so flexible that it can withstand whatever weather buffets and provokes it.

One day we look up and see that our bridge has taken us over to the other side of the garden. We have arrived. We are in that place that seemed so far away when we were digging around in the dead ground of our past, and now suddenly we are here. At first it all looks overwhelming; where do we start? How do we make sense of this new beginning? We become afraid; afraid that we might mess it up, kill it off, spoil it before we have even had a chance to make it the beautiful place we know it could be. But we have built our bridge. We don't have to fall any more. We have crossed over and we can begin to transform ourselves.

To tell a new story about ourselves we can choose whatever we like, for we are now telling a new narrative about our lives. Whatever we want, we can choose it now, by asking ourselves these two important questions: 'Who am I being?' and 'Who do I want to be?'

'Who am I being *right now*?' It is worth taking another moment to think about this important aspect of relating to ourselves (perhaps refer back to your journal notes). This question is not the same as, 'Who am I?' which is an unhelpful question because we are so many different people in the course of one day, and many aspects of who we are derive from the context we find ourselves in. Often, we don't always know definitively who we are, and that is just fine because we can ask ourselves instead this much more skilful question, 'Who am I being?'

'Who am I being *in this moment*?' might be answered with: 'I am being upset', 'I am being angry' or, 'I am being tired.'

This question allows us to identify what we feel and helps us to discover why we feel the way we do. We might be upset because we have just had a row with our partner or friend; we might be angry because we feel they didn't listen to us. We might then realise that we are tired because it is the end of a long day and perhaps now wasn't the most helpful time to have the conversation that led to the row.

By making these distinctions in asking ourselves, 'Who am I being right now?' we can take responsibility for who we are without fear and shame. As we have discovered, it is normal and healthy to have our feelings. It isn't helpful, however, to stay with them if they are hurting ourselves or others.

Again, revisiting the next question, 'Who do I want to be?' allows us to focus on what we need to do next. The more aware we are of who we want to be in any moment, the more likely we are to actualise it. Do we have to stay upset, angry or tired? Does it help us to stay with these feelings? Probably not. So this question can shift us into more promising territory. It could lead us to say, 'I don't want to feel upset or angry with my partner or friend, and I need to relax and rest so I can have a good day tomorrow. Who I want to be right now involves showing understanding to myself and the person I care about. Who I want to be right now is balanced and skilful. Who I want to be right now is loving and caring.'

We can then take ownership of our feelings, share them, if that will help, and move into a more constructive dialogue, which might even include leaving the issue until you are both in a more balanced frame of mind to explore it further. Most problems in relating involve issues that cannot be resolved perfectly, because we are all individuals, entitled to our own point of view. Instead of constantly trying to take control and fix everything to suit ourselves, we can accept and tolerate the reality that there will always be differences. The more we ask ourselves, 'Who am I being?' the more we appreciate who we really are. We can then ask ourselves the exciting question, 'Now, who do I want to be?' In this way we create a process where, instead of staying stuck, we can transform, crossing over to where something more constructive may occur; where we feel we have been able to make a difference.

I hope the work we have done has created a place where you can think about yourself differently. When we have arrived at a point where we can authentically say, 'I accept that I did not have the past I wanted, but that is OK because I can create for myself in each moment a present that makes sense to me, and that will build strong and constructive foundations for a future that I will truly love', then we have much to celebrate.

Daring to be you is about letting go of anything that has constrained you, held you back, made you doubt yourself and left you wondering why you couldn't be the person you thought you really were. Daring to be you is about discarding all the negative messages – real or imagined – that have never helped any of us become the people we want to be. Daring to be you is about creating for ourselves new narratives that move us closer to who and where we want to be in life. Daring to be you is about not judging yourself or other people, and not caring how other people judge you; because you love yourself enough to know that you are doing your best and your best is good enough.

If you want to be curious and experiment with your life, then that is just fine. If you want to live your life differently from those around you and you are not harming anyone in the process, then that is also just fine. If you want to express yourself with freedom and spontaneity, and you know and value yourself and the life that surrounds you deeply, all the better.

As we explored at the beginning of the book, there are no rules in life except the ones we and society impose upon ourselves. The rules of society are there to protect the majority and in the main – in our culture – they attempt to be fair. The rules we impose upon ourselves are often the real problem when it comes to our emotional wellbeing. If this is the case, then let the rules we create be ones that nurture and encourage us, not condemn and hold us back. If we are to have any rules at all, let them be ones that are about love, nurturance, core values, self-worth, and reminding yourself of who you really want to be in each and every moment. Abusing ourselves through cruel and damaging thought processes and behaviours is just as reprehensible as abusing someone else; we wouldn't do it to another person, so why do we allow it in ourselves?

Draw a large circle in your journal and fill it with all the words that tell the story of who you no longer want to be. Don't hold back; put everything in there that you have ever hated about yourself or your life, anything that you have felt upset about or regretted that has caused you pain. Within this circle will appear the core beliefs you have about yourself that hold you back. You will begin to see patterns emerging of self-sabotage, masochism and neglect. Stories of unworthiness, of not being lovable, of being a failure. It won't make a pretty picture, so don't be surprised if you feel sad or anxious as you fill in the old story of your life that needs to be both challenged and treated with compassion.

Now draw another circle. This time fill it with everything you have ever valued about yourself and your life. Note the things you care about, the people you love, the experiences you have had that felt good, fulfilling and worthwhile. Identify what has moved and inspired you. Put in this circle the adventures you have had; the moments of tenderness or closeness that you have achieved, the relationships that resonate for you, the events that have changed you or taken you into a deeper level of understanding. If you have trouble filling the circle, ask someone close to you to help you; they will be able to describe what they value in you, if you find it hard to put it into words yourself.

Now draw a third circle. In this circle place everything that you want to be. Ask yourself the simple question, 'Who do I want to be right now?' and respond to it without censure, without judgement and with compassionate love. There are no right and wrong responses to this exercise. Imagine the qualities, values and meaning that are important to you and which you would like to inhabit for yourself. It could be that you want to be more loving, more generous, less anxious, more forgiving, more patient, less demanding or conflictual. It could be that you want to have more fun, pursue more pastimes that give you pleasure, or create a healthier work life balance. Put anything into this circle that you want in your life.

Now compare the three circles. Notice how you feel when you look at each. Again, do not judge yourself for what you feel; just notice the feelings as they arise in you, name them and let them go. Having contemplated these three worlds, choose which ones you want to keep. I am hoping that you won't want to keep the first, except perhaps as a reminder of the traps you can fall into. If you do, ask yourself: why? Is it really helpful for you to want to stay in a world where you doubt and condemn yourself? It is not the sum of you, it isn't the whole story, and it isn't the truth or essence of who you really are.

The next two circles represent what you value in yourself now, and what you are aiming for in the future. These are worth keeping and represent the bridge into your future. The second circle reminds you of what is important, what nurtures you, and what helps you keep a balanced perspective when the doubts creep back in, as they inevitably will. It is there as a foundation for your new story, helping you to invest in what really matters to you, reminding you of what is meaningful and satisfying. It is a reminder that you are more, so much more, than the negative story you might have been telling about yourself. It is a template for creating the life you really want to live, and a reminder that you can start living that life right now, by staying close to the values and beliefs that are constructive.

The third circle is your map to where you want to get to. It will guide you when you come up against difficulties. It will reassure you that you are still on course, even when life doesn't immediately deliver what you want. It will prevent you getting lost and ending up back in that first circle of discontent. It is an exciting escape route from the old tired narrative of your life and will help you move closer, every day, to who you really want to be. It is the code for creating your reality. If you imagine it, you give it life. If you think of what is possible, you begin to see ways of getting to where you want to go.

The first circle was all about telling you how you couldn't be who you want to be or have what you want in your life. The second circle is a reality check, reminding you that you are so much more than you realise, and that it is vitally important and healthy to value yourself, to give yourself the emotional strength to pursue your life in the most constructive way possible. The third circle is the signpost to where you want to go. We all need goals in life; without any, life is very confusing. But do not worry if there isn't anything concrete to aim for in this circle. That will come in time. What is important is that you have given yourself the opportunity to learn to create your reality, and in this way you can transcend the old you and cross over to the new you.

There is a beautiful Mahayana meditation[17] where we can observe that everything we need is available to us right here and now. We can imagine our potential, and that of all the world, as being like liquid gold, flowing pure and clear. Our anxieties, our defences, our vulnerabilities can obscure it temporarily; but no thought or action, however self-limiting, can completely deny our ability to spontaneously well up with joy, connecting with the infinite possibilities of being alive. This meditation allows us to stay in contact with the philosophy central to this book. Everything flows and everything changes; there is always some action, some path we can explore, to gently move us away from a feeling of being

[17] Claxton, G. (Ed) (1996) *Beyond Therapy: The Impact of Eastern Traditions on Psychological Theory and Practice*. Guernsey Press Ltd.

stuck, transforming us into an unlimited potential of dynamic resolution. If we stay in the world of compassion, we create a fluid existence where anything and everything is possible.

The gift of transformation will always lie within ourselves. Let us not demand that life be good to us, but commit, instead, to being good to life: leaving a legacy worthy of anyone's existence. In being beautiful, true and kind to yourself, you will also be beautiful, true and kind to life. The greatest gift of all is to love and be loved; love your life and it will love you back. You now have your template. Continue to develop a good relationship with yourself; it is, after all, a life-long adventure of exploration. Now, take a deep breath, look up and dare to be your wonderful, unique, amazing self.

### Instants

If I were able to live my life anew,
In the next I would try to commit more errors.
I would not try to be so perfect, I would relax more.
I would be more foolish than I've been,
In fact, I would take few things seriously.
I would be less hygienic.
I would run more risks,
take more vacations,
contemplate more sunsets,
climb more mountains, swim more rivers.
I would go to more places where I've never been,
I would eat more ice cream and fewer beans,
I would have more real problems and less imaginary ones.

I was one of those people that lived sensibly
and prolifically each minute of his life.
Of course I had moments of happiness.
If I could go back I would try
to have only good moments.

Because if you didn't know, life is made
only of moments. Don't lose the now.

I was one of those that never
went anywhere without a thermometer,
a hot-water bottle,
an umbrella, and a parachute.
If I could live again, I would travel lighter.

If I could live again,
I would begin to walk barefoot from the beginning of spring
and I would continue barefoot until autumn ends.
I would take more cart rides,
contemplate more dawns,
and play with more children,
if I had another life ahead of me.

But already you see, I am 85,
and I know that I am dying.

Jorge Luis Borges
*(His own translation)*

# 10

# Additional and Advanced Work

This chapter offers additional exercises, reframes, advice and useful resources for you to continue the work you have started. It also offers advice for those living with someone who is suffering from low mood. I use many of these exercises in my work with patients and in the main they have been adapted from cognitive, mindfulness and compassion-based techniques, which have been well researched as being helpful in clinical trials.

Dip into this chapter whenever you feel you want to deepen your practice, work through a particularly thorny issue or want to explore more of your internal world. Always approach the exercises or advice with an open and curious mind. As with all the exercises in this book, if one or more works particularly well for you, include them in your general wellbeing practice to maintain your sense of connection with yourself, your goals and your ability to truly be yourself.

## Free yourself from your past

Overcoming trauma from your childhood or adolescence can be particularly challenging because developmentally we simply do not have the cognitive (thinking) or emotional maturity to make sense of our experience as an adult would.

Acceptance of our past is not a passive resignation of what has gone before: it is radical in that it is assertive, acknowledging our suffering and losses, whilst compassionately embracing these feelings and in so doing, alleviating the distress our history has caused us.

Ask yourself these questions and write your responses in your journal:

- Can I let go of the hurt my past has caused me?
- Can I let myself step into the present moment free of the hurt my past has caused me?

If you feel unable to set yourself free from the past after exploring these exercises, do not judge yourself; it might be that you need more time to revisit some of the exercises and work through your feelings. You might want help from a trusted friend or family member who can offer alternative perspectives and insights as to where and why you feel stuck. Remember that you have carried these feelings for a lifetime, so they are not necessarily going to change immediately and there are some things that you might have to work through several times before you can come to a place of resolution. Always be gentle with yourself, remind yourself that compassion for your feelings and for your experience is vital if you are to overcome the challenges of your early years and eventual freedom from your past.

**Forgiving**

I would like to write a brief note on forgiving. This is only a note because I do not feel it is my place to tell anyone to forgive. That is something that has to be the individual's choice, and being preached at when someone is feeling a terrible loss that may to them always remain unforgiveable, is crass in the extreme. I do believe that forgiveness can be arrived at after working through the acknowledgement and acceptance stages of transformation, but forgiveness may be something that comes much later on for some of us, even if we have acknowledged and accepted our past. There are some psychological benefits to forgiving, however, that might be helpful to think about.

The ability to forgive leaves us less angry, less stressed, more optimistic and generally feeling healthier. Forgiveness is an altruistic gift, one that frees us from our guilt, so remembering how it feels to be forgiven can enable us to forgive others. It helps to commit to forgiving, to make it a conscious act which we actively hold on to, reminding ourselves that to forgive is to transcend to a place of healing and compassion.

At some point, all of us have to accept that we might not have had the childhood, the family, the parents, the education, the advantages, the past that we desired or deserved. Once we have accepted this, we can move forward into a future where we begin to nurture the potential that is within us to create the life for ourselves that we want to live now.

No longer dragging our past into our future allows us to inhabit the present. And it is within the present moment that everything becomes possible. There is nothing to hold us back, once we have acknowledged this reality. Nothing at all, except of course, ourselves.

## Advanced work on forgiveness

You might want to have someone with you when you do this exercise, particularly if you feel easily overwhelmed or frightened by the event. If you do this exercise alone, make sure you are carefully monitoring your feelings and if you need help, that you have someone you can reach out to, either in person or by phone. It is important that you are not left confused and lost in your emotions and having another mind on hand to maintain a balanced perspective is important if we are to transcend the upset feelings and move into a more tranquil place.

First, recall as objectively as possible the event that you feel you cannot forgive. Visualise the event while focusing on your breathing to steady your emotions. Avoid judgemental labelling and self-pity. Then, describe a narrative from which you can begin to empathise with the person you blame. This is challenging, but essential. Examine their actions, reasons, context, emotions and experiences, while remembering that we are all capable of behaving unthinkingly, sometimes with catastrophic consequences. Meditate on what you have discovered and reflect on whether it helps you in any way to hold on to the feelings that are negative and destructive. The more in touch with your compassionate self you can be, the less you will want to stay with what hurts and the more you will want to let go and transcend.

## How to help someone who is suffering from low mood and negative thinking

Low mood with persistent negativity is not like an ordinary illness located inside our bodies, it is a cognitive and emotional experience of how we relate to ourselves and our world. This means that if we are attempting to care for someone with symptoms of low mood and negative thinking, the ordinary 'convalescing' rules do not apply. Often, being with someone who is low and anxious can make us feel both helpless and alone. We feel we cannot change anything, let alone help, especially when the person we care about is sometimes hurtful and cruel, resentful and jealous of us going about our normal daily routines and can often seem resolutely determined to resist offers of assistance or comfort. Our feelings often become confused with sympathy, but also anger and frustration that nothing seems to make a difference. This can lead to guilt, which in turn can end up making us feel down and lack the motivation to instigate helpful changes.

Dorothy Rowe in *Depression: The Way Out of Your Prison*, perceptively reminds us that if we are living with someone who has symptoms of depression and we want to help them overcome those symptoms, we have to let them change, and for that to happen we too must change. So what changes can we make that will be meaningful and maintain a focus for recovery that is achievable? I have focused on the key areas that need addressing if we are to cope with living with someone who suffers from chronic negative thinking.

Step 1 is comprised of two somewhat paradoxical stages. The first stage of Step 1 is that we need to remind ourselves that, as adults, we are ultimately responsible for our own happiness. The second stage of Step 1 is that the one guaranteed way of achieving lasting happiness is to be attentive to other people's happiness and wellbeing. This clearly is paradoxical, yet in order to help ourselves, we need to help others, whether we are feeling depressed, anxious, happy or sad. The more we do for others, the happier we feel in ourselves.

To help someone who is suffering from chronic negativity we must first understand that we are responsible for our own happiness, as they are responsible for theirs. This first step serves to remind us that we are not the problem and that it is not our fault that they are depressed. We must then ensure we make time to regenerate ourselves and replenish our reserves if we are focusing our attention away from ourselves. By taking care of our own wellbeing, we will have the energy to focus compassionate attention on our depressed loved one.

Step 2 is to remind ourselves and those we care about who are depressed, that in Rowe's words, which echo those of the Buddha's, 'It is not what happens to us which matters but how we interpret what happens to us.' When our depressed partner or friend frequently interprets events negatively, we can gently remind them that this is but one point of view that perhaps is largely perceived through a filter of depression. We can suggest that there are other perspectives to be considered, some that perhaps are more balanced and that, in choosing an alternative perspective, they might feel differently about the event and therefore themselves. It is important not to tell them that they are wrong, or that their view is incorrect, as this will reinforce their feelings of inadequacy and provoke a circular argument, which confounds you both. This gentle reminder that there are many different potential inter-pretations usefully promotes a healthy curiosity as to what else might be occurring. This in turn can shift a mood into something less negative and more balanced.

Step 3 is to remind ourselves that what is obvious to us as

a helpful strategy to aid recovery might not be at all obvious to someone with depression. We might see very clearly that exercising would be highly beneficial in lifting a negative mood state. We might not see what a huge effort this might be to someone who feels depressed and who, through the negative lens of their depression, can see no point in doing anything to help themselves at all. When this arises, it is important to again show compassion and understanding, but also remind them that until they try something different they will stay stuck. The steep slope to recovery is traversed by taking small steps, tiny 'risks', to see if something different can occur.

Where you can help is to break down the task into manageable steps, so that they do not feel overwhelmed. For example, instead of saying, 'You need to take some exercise in order to get better', you could say 'Why don't we walk down to the shop through the park together?' Instead of saying 'You should get up and go to the gym', you could say 'Let's go to the gym today and choose one exercise machine and see if we can stay on it for ten minutes.'

The amount of patience you can generate will depend on whether you are looking after your own wellbeing. Remember that you too need restorative, replenishing, energising activities that you can store up to get you through a tough day living with someone who feels depressed. Take time out when you feel your patience sapping, go for a walk, meet up with a friend, luxuriate in a warm bath and listen to some favourite music. Remember, you do not need to be with them twenty-four hours a day; you need a break if you are to be of any help. Remind yourself of the first step, that ultimately we are all responsible for our own happiness. If your patience is ebbing and you are feeling trapped by their depression, take a weekend away. Patience is a virtue, but it will not do either of you any good if you become a martyr to it.

Remember that there are roles in depression, the role of 'sufferer' and that of 'care-taker'. These are very potent and can become rigidly fixed, preventing both you and them from changing. Think about the roles you have taken on and see if you can do anything differently to loosen them to allow a more flexible, responsive way of relating to each other. Do you worry that if they cease to be depressed then you will have less control over them? Do you think if they were to stop being depressed that you might become depressed instead? Does their depression give you a raison d'être? How would it feel to you if they were to be happy? Is it something you want or fear?

Help them separate the depression from themselves. Remind them that their negativity isn't really them; it is the depression speaking ('that's not really you, that's depression talking'). This will enable both of you to find new and healthier ways of relating to the symptoms. Encourage them to read this book, or other books that offer tools and techniques in overcoming the punishing grind that is daily low mood. There are alternatives, it doesn't have to be this way. Little by little, with encouragement, everyone has the capacity to change, regardless of circumstance. It is just about seeing things differently, making different decisions and choosing wisely.

### Remembering remembering?

Sometimes we can become caught up in remembering painful past events with an almost obsessional ferocity. We end up feeling very low, sad, upset and distressed by these remembered thoughts. Labelling ruminations about the past as 'remembering remembering' is a helpful mindfulness technique that can allow you to identify what is happening to your thinking. When you remind yourself that you are 'remembering remembering' you give yourself the opportunity to observe what is arising in you by bearing witness to your experience.

First, identify your thoughts as remembering past events and label them as 'remembering remembering'. This can help you to identify yourself with the objective witness of these disturbing thoughts rather than identifying yourself as a depressed or damaged person trapped in a destructive way of thinking.

When you adopt the position of a witness, you can see more clearly that you are remembering a painful event, an event that took place in the past and which is dominating your present. You can then label it objectively as 'remembering remembering' without being seduced into being caught up in the painful drama of the experience. The witness position can create psychological distance between the 'you' who experiences the painful event and the 'you' who is presently remembering it.

The more we bear witness to our suffering, the less likely we are to get caught up in the drama of it all. This gives us more power in creating a more compassionate, yet objective perspective that allows us to shift our position where our energies are not dissipated on cruel ruminations which cannot be resolved and leave us feeling disconnected from what is possible in our lives.

Allow your witness to guide you in your response to your

thinking. Let your witness become a compassionate best friend who wants to help you see things differently. Listen to the voice of your witness as it helps you connect with the compassionate part of yourself that does not want to stay stuck in this painful way of thinking. Write down in your journal your experience of identifying and labelling your thinking in this way. Reflect on how it can help you. How are you now left feeling? How else can developing a compassionate witness help you?

## Already Always Listening Exercise

'Already always listening' is a way of describing how we listen to someone yet all the while we're making assumptions about what they are saying without really listening to them, based on past conversations and experiences. This can mean that we get into arguments, misunderstandings or other unhelpful ways of communicating because we make judgements and assumptions that separate us from the present moment, taking us to previous conversations that are irrelevant and unhelpful to us now. To break the habit, try this exercise with someone whom you have begun to feel stuck with when communicating:

Say something like, 'Talk to me about what is going on for you and I promise not to interrupt you. When you have finished I will feedback to you what I think I have heard and you can let me know if I have heard you correctly.' When they have finished, feedback to them and then let them tell you what they have heard you say and whether that was what they meant. Then swap roles and repeat the exercise. Take some time to discuss with each other what you both heard and understood from each other and discuss whether that has made a difference to the way in which you have communicated.

Practise this exercise and use it particularly when you have important issues to discuss so that they don't become heated, angry or upset. If you find that you are still in a place of distress even after doing the exercise, then both of you should take time out and come back to it later and try again.

## Help with acknowledging and accepting your emotions without acting them out

These steps are adapted from Marsha Linehan's Dialectical Behavioural Therapy, mentioned earlier, which combines Eastern philosophy and Western behavioural therapy, and has been very successful among people who suffer from mood instability. First, observe the emotion as it arises in you, noting its presence. Give yourself space to step back, using the breathing space or the breathing technique 'let go'. Unstick yourself from the emotion by naming it for what it is, such as 'This is my fear, distress, pain, upset, anger . . .' or whatever the emotion is.

Now, experience your emotion as a wave rising and falling within. Do not attempt to block or suppress what you are feeling or try to get rid of it or push it away. Observe it for what it is and know that it will pass.

Remind yourself that your emotions only take ninety seconds to be released and flood through the body and are then dispersed. You don't need to try and keep the emotion around, or hold on to it or amplify it by ruminating on it or dredging up past experiences where you felt this way before. Your emotions are designed to flow rapidly through you and if you simply observe them and then let them go, this is exactly what will happen.

Gently remind yourself that you are not your emotion. You do not need to act on your emotion and now is a good moment to remember times when you have felt differently. We can love our emotions, whatever they may be, as they are a reminder that we are not disconnected from ourselves but are engaged in our lives. Judging our emotions does not help us, and if we are willing we can radically accept what we are feeling and then let it go. The more we do this, the more our emotions will flow fluidly through us without us having to act out on them unskilfully.

### Skills to Reframe Your Experience of Fear, Guilt and Anger

**Fear**

If you frequently experience fear or anxiety, these simple strategies will help you regain a more balanced perspective. Whatever you are afraid of doing, keep doing it repeatedly until it no longer transfixes you. Do not avoid people, places, activities, events, animals, or any other stimulus that you are afraid of. Actively commit to approaching them until you reduce your fear. Avoidance is not a skilful strategy for living life; it leads to a narrowing of our experience and a shutting down and disconnection from our lives. Whenever you approach what you fear, reward yourself with an activity that develops your sense of control and mastery. If you feel overwhelmed, make a list of small steps or goals that are more manageable, then do the first thing on the list. Use the change plan to guide you.

## Guilt

Many people feel guilty for 'everything', often in the absence of ever having done anything really bad. Some even feel guilty for being alive, particularly if they have lost a loved one. An overarching sense of guilt pervades our sense of self and all our activities, meaning that we feel we do not deserve to really let go and enjoy ourselves. Our unrealistic guilt leaves us judging and condemning ourselves, often with a mantra of 'I don't deserve to be happy/content/successful/in love' or whatever it is we feel we should deny ourselves because guilt is telling us that we are undeserving.

Paradoxically, however, it is generally good people who feel guilty. The people who should feel remorse are probably too busy acting mindlessly and too lacking in insight to feel guilty about themselves. It is helpful to remind ourselves when we are feeling guilty that it is because we are basically a good person with a conscience, who doesn't want to hurt, upset or be unfair to anyone else.

Another important thing about guilt is that it is pointless, except perhaps as an emotional barometer. Staying guilty doesn't help you and doesn't help the person you are feeling guilty about. Some people would go so far as to say that it is the most selfish of emotions. This is somewhat harsh; we are in danger here of feeling guilty about feeling guilty! There are two kinds of guilt: the 'futile' kind and the legitimate 'make amends' kind. This gives us two choices in how we deal with our guilt. If we have done something to feel legitimately guilty about, we need to make amends for it, clear it up and move on. When we make a mess, we don't leave it to someone else to clear up, we mop it up – or at least that is what the responsible and respectful position demands. This is what we should do with 'make amends' guilt. If you have made a mistake with someone, apologise, put as much right as you can, and learn from it. Staying guilty doesn't do anything except lower our self-esteem. Apologising and making amends leaves us feeling better. Staying guilty is paralysing; acting on it is liberating.

If you really cannot make amends for something that you have done, then learn from it and resolve not to do this thing again. Accept that you cannot clear up the mess and move on, reminding yourself that staying guilty is pointless and that you are only human and therefore fallible. We all make mistakes. We can forgive ourselves by showing ourselves some understanding.

The second type of guilt is futile guilt and this is rather more complex. This is the sort of guilt that often originates in our childhoods and which we have taken on from our parents, teachers or religious leaders' hang-ups. Examples such as: feeling guilty for enjoying sex, for enjoying ourselves and having fun, for doing things for ourselves, or feeling guilty when we say 'no' to someone.

For example, if we have a tendency to constantly look after others and cannot say no to people, that compulsion to please often stems from being taught that pleasing ourselves is selfish and 'bad'. So, if you are feeling guilty about saying 'no', ask yourself this: in saying no, are you establishing an important boundary that is protective and in reality maintains your own wellbeing? If so, drop the guilt. This is futile guilt, not based in reality at all. You are no longer a child, but an adult who is allowed to have an opinion and develop their own way of doing things.

Similarly, if you are someone who can never really enjoy yourself because somewhere deep inside you feel guilty for finding pleasure in things, think back to where you learned this joyless lesson. Many of us will have been exposed to doctrines that condemn enjoyment and pleasure as weaknesses or faults. They are not. Being able to enjoy ourselves, have fun, relax, take time out and generally have a good time are essential ingredients in leading a healthy, balanced and nurturing life. If we deny ourselves these important things, we become depressed, envious, bitter and moribund.

Guilt at feeling pleasure is a complex intra-personal dynamic, which needs a serious talking to. Ask yourself why you are not allowed to have fun when other people do, and clearly derive pleasure and regeneration from the experience? It is often in these periods of recreation that we have our best ideas, our most useful insights and our Eureka! moments (that one we all know happened in a bath – how deliciously relaxing!). Driving ourselves all the time because we feel guilty if we stop just leads to burn-out and self-induced misery. Shake off this crazy guilt any way you can. It is sapping your creativity, your lust for life and your chance to indulge yourself in activities that are healthy and life-enhancing. Next time you feel the clammy hand of guilt trying to strangle the fun out of you, gently tell it to get lost, as it is no longer welcome in your life. It is of no use, it does not help and it certainly doesn't encourage emotional growth. Instead of saying to yourself, 'I feel guilty if I do x, y or z,' say instead, 'Go get the fun' and see how differently you feel by giving yourself permission to be you and do what you really want to do.

## Anger

Anger is an important human emotion. It tells us when an injustice, something wrong or an imbalance has occurred that needs to be remedied. Learning to be assertive rather than 'acting out' our anger allows us to identify what has gone wrong without resorting to hostility, attack or other unhelpful generalisations. Here are the most common forms of expressing anger:

| *Assertive communication reflects:* | *Aggressive communication reflects:* |
|---|---|
| I count. | I count. |
| You count. | You don't count. |
| *Passive–Aggressive communication reflects:* | *Passive communication reflects:* |
| I count. | I don't count. |
| You don't count, but I'm not going to tell you this. | You count. |

Passive aggression is a style of communication arising when we don't acknowledge or express our anger, instead holding it all inside while acting passively on the surface. Passive aggression leaks out insidiously, however, with bitterness, recriminations and taking on a 'martyr' role. We can resort to covert punishments – punishing someone behind their back – to make ourselves feel better and to seek revenge.

Alice Domar in her helpful book *Self-Nurture* describes being passive as when we want to take the psychological path of least resistance. Being passive and denying our feelings can make us feel worthless, guilty, anxious, and physically ill, affecting our emotional life generally. By denying we have any feelings, we end up unable to be intimate or emotionally honest with others, leaving us feeling abandoned and isolated.

Assertiveness is a skill that we can use to control the way we use our anger. Instead of trying to punish those we perceive as having wronged us, we attempt with skilful communication to have our needs acknowledged and met. We usually first become aware of our anger as a surge of energy coursing through our body, that 'rush of blood to the head' feeling that leaves us feeling hot and hostile. Acting without thinking on this aggressive feeling we can put ourselves and others in danger. Here is Dr Domar's method of slowing down this aggressive response so that we can reflect on what is happening and then choose to do something far more constructive than blowing a fuse.

First        STOP

Then              BREATHE

Then                    REFLECT

Then                          CHOOSE

This will give you time to consider the most effective and assertive words and actions possible.

For example, let's say you have arranged for your partner or flatmate to meet you at the supermarket as you will have heavy shopping bags to bring home that will benefit you both. Later, while you are at the shop, they call to say they are delayed at work and will not be able to meet you there at the arranged time. A reactive response would be to feel upset and angry. The thoughts might be, 'You don't support me, you are always so selfish.' You may shout at them (aggressive) or when you see them not speak to them or feel hostile (passive aggressive).

Alternatively, you could reduce the amount you buy so you can manage bringing it home on your own, and when you return you could sit down with your partner or flatmate and describe your feelings. You could say something like, 'I really wanted you to come and help me and I felt let down when you didn't. As you can probably imagine, it was hard work bringing those bags back on my own.' In this way, you own your experience, you tell it how it was without rancour and you get to express your real feelings without resorting to aggression or passive aggression. This method of communication is far better for our emotional health while also encouraging increased understanding and clearer communication generally, which can only be a good thing.

### Identifying Relapse Signatures

It would, of course, be a mistake to think that just because you have completed the workshops in this book you will never feel distress again. It is more a question of learning better ways to take care of ourselves when distressing situations arise, so that we can navigate through them with less fear and rigidity. This is not about becoming hyper-vigilant to our upsets, but gently becoming more aware of our vulnerabilities and then taking care of them.

The common signs that our resources are low and our wellbeing bank is overdrawn include: irritability, decreasing social participation, change in sleep and eating habits, fatigue, giving up exercise, not wanting to open letters or pay bills, postponing deadlines, and feeling hopeless. You may have more that are personal to you. Jot them down in your journal so that you have a clear sense of when you may need to invest more carefully in your wellbeing.

Additionally, ask yourself, 'What in the past has prevented me from noticing and attending to my feelings, for example: pushing away, denial, distraction, self-medication with alcohol, arguments, blaming others?' Again, note your responses in your journal. Now ask yourself, 'How can I include other family members or friends in my early-warning system for detecting the signs or a relapse?' Once you have identified the ways in which you can improve your support network, enlist the help of your family and friends by sharing what you have learned and explaining to them how their input will protect you and prevent a relapse. Remember that altruism is a precious gift and by being open about your needs, they will be able to respond with compassion and support and get to feel good about themselves as well!

## Action Plan for Relapse Prevention
If you are beginning to feel overwhelmed with negativity, anxiety or hopelessness, take a breathing space and connect with your practice, that is whatever you have discovered has really helped you throughout the eight weeks of workshops that you continue to use. Perhaps refer to your journal as a reminder of what has proved most useful in the past and what you have worked through before that can help you again now. Gently reflect that the feelings may be very intense at this moment, but what you need now is no different from what you have practised before.

Now do something, especially some action that in the past

would have given you a sense of pleasure and mastery, even if it seems futile to do so right now. Break down these activities into smaller parts so that they feel manageable to you. Feel free to complete only a part of the task, or only doing it for a short period of time. After you have done as much as you feel able to manage, in your journal ask yourself these helpful questions:

- How can I best be kind to myself right now?
- What is the best gift I can give myself in this moment?
- I don't know how long this mood will last, so how can I best look after myself until it passes?

In time, the feelings will subside, particularly if you do not ruminate on them or let your internal judge get the better of you. Once they have subsided, reward yourself with something nurturing, like a deep, warm and fragranced bath, or a stroll around your nearest park. Repeat this process until the crisis is over and once again you become grounded in a reality that allows you to heal and start again. Choose to take care of your feelings and commit to choosing to take care of them over and over, until it becomes automatic, even if you have to start again moment by moment.

**How to Nurture Yourself Further**
Taking your feelings seriously is not about indulging them but about looking after them constructively. Here are some more techniques that will encourage you to look after your mind and body, ensuring that your wellbeing bank is positively invested in, allowing you to take out dividends whenever you need to.

Massage is a therapeutic treatment with many physical and emotional health benefits, positively influencing the nervous system. It can be invigorated and stimulating, or relaxing and calming. Our brain releases endorphins in response to the skin being stroked, and these soothe the outer and inner body. Massage stimulates the lymphatic system, which expels toxins built up through pollution, alcohol and poor diet. It also improves blood circulation, boosts the immune system, relieves stress and pain, normalises blood pressure, balances the emotions and much more. Qualified massage practitioners can be found at www.massagetherapy.co.uk. Touch, including massage, is essential for your psychological wellbeing; aim for a minimum of seven physical contacts every day with a consenting person, or pet.

I have already discussed the benefits of music as a mood enhancer. Likewise, dancing lifts the spirits. When we dance we immerse ourselves in a joyful, harmonious sensory experience, stimulating our eyes, ears and touch. Dance takes many different forms; there really is something for everyone, from formal dances such as tango, salsa, ballroom and ballet, to informal disco and clubbing. However old you are, keep on dancing, bringing zest to your social life while at the same time getting exercise and releasing those vital endorphins essential for a happy mind. Dancing regularly reduces your risk of illness, such as cardiovascular disease, high blood pressure and adult onset diabetes.

Plan a 'No TV' night, at least twice a week. On your 'No TV' evenings you can go out with friends, take a course in something that you have been wanting to explore or go and see something amazing in the arts or join a book club to feed your soul. Nurture yourself by exploring real life, where you can invest in yourself, rather than the fake one you see on TV that can make you feel disaffected, passive and numbed out. If you feel really brave, cut out TV altogether; after a few days you will not miss it and after a few months you will not want it back in your life, as you free up hours of time that you can devote to activities, pastimes, friends and challenges that give you feelings of real pleasure and mastery in your life.

Consider a news diet (as promoted by Dr Andrew Weil in his classic *8 Weeks to Optimum Health*). Being addicted to news bulletins can leave us feeling anxious with that persistent unbalanced focus on negative, shocking, distressing and tragic world events. Very soon we begin to feel that everything is out of control, including ourselves. This is not to say we should be uninformed about the world, but we can ensure that we do not gorge ourselves on stress-inducing news fixes that can leave us feeling overwhelmed. Try cutting out news media one day a week and, if you like the benefits, increase your news diet to several days a week. Alternatively, if you really feel the need to stay informed for whatever reason, limit yourself to only one source of news once a day.

Many of us work over fifty hours a week, regardless of the type of work we do. We work some of the longest hours in the world and there are no advantages to our health or wellbeing in doing so – quite the opposite, in fact. To create a healthy work–life balance, impose these healthy boundaries to make a clear distinction between what is your work life and what is your home life. Don't take work home with you (unless, of course, you work from home); leave it at the office where it belongs. Likewise, don't make work calls in your personal time. If you can work flexible or part-time hours, reduce your commute and make it a more pleasant experience by travelling off-peak. We can be incredibly productive when the office or work place is quiet, and arriving early means you can leave early to exercise, take a class, view a gallery or meet with friends. Work only the hours that you are employed for, and if this feels impossible, make sure you leave work on time at least three evenings a week. Happy people live longer. And remember, no one has 'I wish I had stayed later in the office' as their epitaph.

## Psychotherapy

If you have found the techniques in this book helpful and would like to explore your internal world further, therapy is a form of self-nurturing that can divest us of our anxieties, neuroses and low mood and help us work towards a more balanced and constructive future. Your GP can refer you to a psychologist working in the NHS, or there are two professional associations for private psychotherapy that can assist you in finding a qualified therapist. If CBT is not for you, do not despair. There are other forms of talking therapy that might suit you better. If you would like to explore your past, particularly focusing on your parental relationships, you might find a psychodynamic approach more useful. This type of therapy works with how you respond to your therapist in what is called the transference. You can read more about this approach on my website: www.drceciliadfelice.com. If your children are experiencing behavioural or emotional problems because of stressors at home, you might want to try a systemic therapy which looks at the different roles each family member takes and will show

you ways of introducing difference so that the family func-
tions more skilfully. CBT is not a useful therapy for bereavement issues and if you are experiencing a loss of this nature,
then a bereavement counsellor would offer you the space,
time and support to work through your grieving process.

**British Association of Behavioural and Cognitive
Psychotherapies** – *Helpful for phobias, anxiety, depression,
OCD, trauma, PTSD, bi-polar disorder.*
The Globe Centre
PO Box 9
BB5 0XB
United Kingdom
Telephone: 01254 875277
Website: www.babcp.com

**British Association for Counselling and Psychotherapy** –
*Helpful for exploratory work, childhood issues, issues with
parents, life changes, bereavements, abuse.*
BACP House
35–37 Albert Street
Rugby
Warwickshire CV21 2SG
United Kingdom
Email : bacp@bacp.co.uk
Website : www.bacp.co.uk

Do not feel you have to work with the first therapist you
meet. If your therapy is going to have a nurturing effect on
your life, it is important that you feel comfortable, contained
and secure. It is not unusual to meet with several therapists

first, until you are confident you have found the right one for you.

## Additional Resources

David D. Burns, *The Feeling Good Handbook* (ISBN 978–045228132–5). Excellent CBT resource.

Zindel V. Segal, J. Mark G. Williams and John D. Teasdale, *Mindfulness-Based Cognitive Therapy* (ISBN 978–157230706–3). Deepen your knowledge of mindfulness to lift low mood.

Bhante Henepola Gunaratana, *Mindfulness in Plain English* (ISBN 978–086171321–9). Discover the myths, realities and benefits of meditation and the practice of mindfulness.

Alice Domar, *Self-Nurture* (ISBN 978–067088286–1). Inspirational source of self-nurturing techniques for wellbeing specifically aimed at women.

Martin Seligman, *Authentic Happiness* ( ISBN 978–185788329–9). Good for developing strategies to create and maintain positive thinking.

Jeffrey Young, *Re-Inventing Your Life* (ISBN 978–045227204–0). Good for developing more positive and fulfilling relationships.

Jon Kabat-Zinn, *Full Catastrophe Living* (ISBN 978–074991585–8). Good for developing strategies to cope with stress, pain and illness.

Geshe Kelsang Gyatso, *Eight Steps to Happiness* (ISBN 978–0948006623). The Buddhist approach to loving kindness.

Lama Surya Das, *Awakening the Buddha Within* (ISBN 978–0553505375). Beautifully accessible Buddhist wisdom for the Western world.

**Web-Based Resources**

www.moodgym.anu.edu.au – Free interactive CBT programme to help those with depression and/or anxiety to identify and overcome problem emotions and develop good coping skills. Consists of five CBT modules, a personal workbook and feedback evaluation form.

www.depressioncenter.net – Free interactive sixteen-session CBT course, aimed at people with severe depression; offers information on depression, symptom assessment, session diary and online support group.

www.livinglifetothefull.co.uk – Life skills resource. The course has been written by a psychiatrist who has many years of experience using a CBT approach in helping people use these skills in everyday life.

www.mheccu.ubc.ca/publications – Self-care 'Anti-Depressant Skills Workbook', with worksheets and advice on diet, sleep and medication. There is also a version for teenagers.

# Index